Tamed

A City Girl Walks From Mexico To Canada
On The Pacific Crest Trail

ANNE ELIZABETH O'REGAN

Printed in the United States of America

Cover Design & Illustration, Chris Monahan
Text Design, Marie-Anne Gajdosik

ISBN-10: 0-6924-4109-3
ISBN-13: 978-0-692-44109-1

To Beekers, thank you for giving me the space to breathe, write, and flourish within, and without.

To all I have met both on and off the path.

And to my family, friends, and teachers, in deepest gratitude, for the texture, teachings, and richness you have bestowed upon my life.

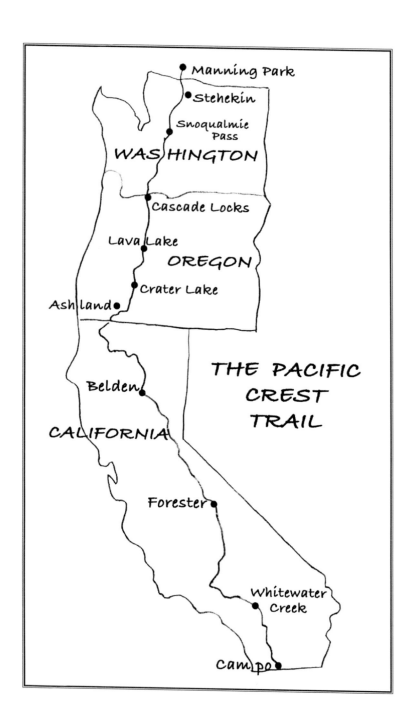

Manning Park

Stehekin

Snoqualmie Pass

WASHINGTON

Cascade Locks

Lava Lake

OREGON

Crater Lake

Ashland

THE PACIFIC CREST TRAIL

Belden

CALIFORNIA

Forester

Whitewater Creek

Campo

1

Campo to Whitewater Creek

We're all just walking each other home.

~ RAM DASS

April 22, 2010

The wall that separates Mexico from the United States looks like the side of a rust-colored freight train, only higher and longer—endless, really. I place my palm on the cold metal, and then go stand with 19 other would-be thru-hikers beside the Pacific Crest Trail monument. Pictures are taken, it starts to rain, and the group disperses as I push open my brand new silver-domed ultra-light umbrella. Every molecule in my body burns with anticipation as I begin to walk. I'm no longer planning this long journey, I'm actually here, surrounded by cacti and fog, slip-sliding on damp red earth, taking my first steps north to Canada. The plan for today is to hike 21 miles to Lake Morena, which is a thought I can easily consider. Harder to consider, *truly consider*, are the 2,629 miles that lie beyond today. What about those miles? Twenty-one miles—not a problem; all the way to Canada—not so sure. Walking thousands of miles into the deep unknown is outside of my comfort zone, but after sitting behind a desk in downtown Boston for over two decades, *outside* is exactly where I want to be.

What will it be like to live in the natural world for months on end? I honestly don't know. The PCT has lured me here to find out. I imagine that if I make it all the way to Canada my body will feel very strong and the accumulated miles of "deep outside" might somehow stay with me, live in me, long after the walk is done. Though the truth is, I have no idea what the next five months, or its after-effects, will teach me.

For as long as I can remember I've been an athlete. Once when I was very young, perhaps three or four, I stepped out of the house and began to run. I ran to the end of our sleepy road to a busy street, took a left and then another. I'd never been this far from home by myself. I felt the breeze on my face and my hair getting tousled and was giddy with delight as my body moved through this exhilarating new world. I ran past yipping dogs and kids playing hopscotch and was startled to see my house through the trees, perched on a distant hill. I kept running. I ran past gardens, and trees, and lilacs that spilled onto the sidewalk and onto me, their fragrance mingling with the air I sucked in, as I ran and ran and ran.

When I finally reached home, I swung open the back door and instinctively knew to keep quiet. Nothing had changed here. My mom was still at the kitchen sink doing dishes, and my little sister was still on the kitchen floor playing with her Kewpie doll. I was stunned they hadn't noticed my absence and as much as I wanted to tell them, I knew it best to remain silent. Otherwise, I may have to spend time in the punishment chair. My exciting adventure remained a secret. No one ever knew, that I knew, at such a young age, the thrill of discovering strange new worlds. And I've been discovering them ever since.

I first learned about the Pacific Crest Trail a year and a half ago, while hiking in the Sierras on the John Muir Trail. When I returned from that trip I started researching the PCT, not that *I* would ever do such a thing. I was just curious. But the more I researched, the more curious I became, until one day, curiosity turned into desire. In a few short weeks the small flame of desire turned into an inferno, and I started to plot my escape from the city. Life was feeling too predictable. It was time to go for a walk. And now, here I am on this April morning, nervous but ready to see where this walk will lead.

What will it be like to hike 700 miles in the desert? Can I even do it? How will I find water? What about snakes? And what about the High Sierras in this record-high snow year, how on earth will I find the trail? Not to mention Northern California, Oregon and remote wild Washington—places I know little about. Plus, how does one sleep outside night after night, in all kinds of weather, for months on end? A part of me feels like it's the most natural thing in the world to want to find out. And that's the part me that got me to the Mexican border, ready to walk thousands of miles north to the Canadian border, and eight miles beyond to Manning Park, British Colombia.

The first few miles wind their way through flat desert then rise and sink behind sage-covered hills. As a crow flies, it's only 1,000 miles from Mexico to Canada. The additional 1,650 miles will accrue from walking a crooked path, and climbing up and down mountains and hills. The fog clears and a few of us walk together among low, thick vegetation, and tall, blooming cacti. I keep a vigilant eye out for snakes but see none. After only four miles I step into a hole, twist my ankle and fall smack down onto the earth.

I quickly get up, wipe the dirt from my knees and think "Ok fine, that's out of the way. This doesn't need to happen again." Meaning, my weak left ankle has just given out and I don't want this to become a habit. I limp along, slowly regaining my composure, until the ache in my swollen ankle lessens and my focus returns to the trail.

Sage, sign and desert hills.

I've never spent time in a desert. My only impressions are from Lawrence of Arabia racing his handsome white horse across vast barren sand dunes. And from Edward Abbey's *Desert Solitaire*, which I read decades ago, and from which I can only remember the topic of venomous snakes. Now that I'm here, I learn right away that deserts are much more than vacant, snaky places. This one is rich in color and teeming with life. Wildflowers abound in every direction, in every shade of pink, purple, and blue. Striped and spotted lizards appear and disappear at my feet. Rabbits bounce by, while hummingbirds dart about in the bushes. All of it—all of this—is mine just for being here. The desert is anything but dull.

I arrive at Lake Morena in mid-afternoon. Hundreds of people are gathered here to celebrate the annual PCT kick-off weekend. This is a huge contrast to the three people I know who have even heard of the trail. Some are here to offer advice, others to sell gear, and some to simply have fun. There's music and food and the mood is festive. I've done my research but still have plenty of questions for those offering advice, like how exactly does one find water in the desert? What's the latest on snow conditions in the Sierras? Any tips about food? And what about those pesky rattlesnakes?

It starts raining again as I pitch my tent under a tree; then walk around meeting people and talking trail. The rain comes down hard. It's too damp and chilly to linger. I head back to my tent and crawl inside. I'll be here for two more nights, there'll be plenty of time for my questions.

Just before leaving home, I made a last minute decision to upgrade my sleeping gear and I'm looking forward to trying it out. Once inside my new bag, it doesn't take long to realize I have a serious problem. It's a 15-degree sleeping bag, which means it's supposed to keep a person warm in temperatures as low as 15. The problem is that it's only 45 degrees at the moment and I can't get warm. To make the bag ultra-light the manufacturers shaved off ounces by reducing loft (amount of down feathers) on one entire side of the bag and by removing the zipper cuff. I knew these things prior to purchase and it all sounded good at the time, but now that I'm actually using the bag, it doesn't work. I'm warmish on one side of my body and freezing on the other, plus there's a steady draft along the length of the bag because of the missing cuff. My new sleeping pad isn't helping matters either because it, too, has little insulation. I can't believe it. How could I have messed up like this? Why didn't I test the gear at home? The pad feels like a slab of ice. I try to remedy the situation by putting on all my clothes: wool cap, another shirt, long pants, a jacket, three pairs of socks, and a pair gloves. It doesn't help. I put every non-wearable item— backpack, maps, guidebooks, writing pad, and running shoes— between the pad and the earth hoping it might help insulate. It doesn't. I squish the sleeping pad into the already mummy-tight bag but this doesn't help either and I start to shiver. How can my very expensive top-of the-line gear not work? Especially when it's not even that cold out? I spend a long sleepless night trying to figure out how to warm up but basically freeze until dawn.

After breakfast, I speak with some onsite gear experts only to learn that my brand new sleeping gear is made for men. I learn that men sleep warmer than women, due to higher resting body temperatures. I consider my options. It's too complicated to get to a city from this outpost. Therefore, I borrow a cell phone (no reception on mine) and arrange to have replacement gear sent 90 miles up the trail, to Warner Springs. A friend from home is letting me borrow his bag, and will have it there waiting for me. One sleepless night turns into three until finally, on Sunday April 24th, under a vibrant blue sky, I hoist my pack onto my shoulders, find the trail and start hiking. All I need to do is walk 90 miles for a warm sleeping bag, just 90 miles—then I can sleep.

Adrenalin is flowing strong as a large group of us hit the trail. This feels like the real start of the hike! The large group splits up into smaller ones and I end up walking with two young guys from the

Northeast: a vegan furniture maker from Vermont who's growing alfalfa sprouts in one of his water bottles (I'm very impressed) and a nonstop talker who's a student at Goddard and is carrying "tarot cards instead of chocolate," implying that he'd rather carry the weight of the deck than the weight of a chunk of dark chocolate. A few miles up the trail he does tarot readings for several hikers. I think we all would have been better off with chocolate.

We take breaks during the day huddling with others alongside thin streams, getting water, and lingering in shade when we can find it. It's a warm day and after 17 miles we start looking for a place to camp. I don't have the nerve to camp solo yet. I need to ease myself into this outdoor world and get used to it first, especially at night. I have dinner and camp with five others, and while they're sleeping soundly, I lie awake shivering for the fourth night in a row. I remind myself that in 73 miles I'll have new gear and that things will be okay. I repeat this mantra over and over throughout the night—just 73 miles and things will be okay. For now, I simply have to get used to the cold and get used to not sleeping.

The next day I see lots of critters: horny toads, California quail, more hummingbirds and several species of lizards. In the hot afternoon, I spread out under a big shade tree and drift into a heavy slumber. Hours later, I wake up feeling refreshed for the first time in almost a week. I reach into my pocket and pull out a piece of purple wampum (quahog shell) plucked from a Cape Cod beach, while on a run a few weeks ago. I've been carrying it with me for good luck. I place it at the base of the tree as a token of gratitude for gifting me with sleep.

The rest of the day is spent walking in and out of sand-colored canyons. When the sharp afternoon light softens, I approach a group of six thru-hikers who've made camp. I want to join them but can't bear the thought of spending yet another cold night in my tent. In order to avoid another painfully long teeth-chattering night, I've decided to night hike. When I mention this to one kind hiker, he offers to share his sleeping bag with me, "Just to help keep you warm," and I honestly believe he means it.

I study the water report that was handed out at the kick-off. It lists water sources and their most recent status with comments such as: "This creek was flowing well on 4/15" or "Turn right at intersection x and walk 30 feet to an unreliable creek. It's usually dry by June." It also notes occasional water caches placed along the trail by locals. I'm directed to a cache a mile past the campers. Hidden in the bushes are a dozen one-gallon jugs filled with clean water. I drink a cup and replenish my water bottle. A half mile later I pass two hikers filling their water bottles from a horse trough and wonder if I'll ever have to do that. This thought is very unappealing.

I've heard about night hiking but never expected I would try it, especially alone. The thought of another miserable night in my tent has given me the courage to try. My plan is to walk until I'm too tired to take another step. If it weren't for my impossible sleeping situation, I would never attempt this, but what have I got to lose? Anything is better than staying awake all night due to the cold.

I walk up a red dirt road in the twilight to a high cliff. There's a plaque nailed to a rock dedicated to a hang glider pilot who took his last flight here. I turn away from the plaque and watch as a giant full moon lifts itself off the eastern horizon and hovers above the endless desert. Night descends as I nervously wander into a silent canyon. What about mountain lions? We saw mountain lion tracks in the mud yesterday, and the UC Davis professor at the kickoff said there are hundreds of them living in Southern California. Who knew? He mentioned they prefer small prey. With that thought in mind, I open my umbrella to make myself appear larger.

A few feet ahead something skitters across the trail and dives into a thicket of chaparral. I tighten my grip on the umbrella and walk tenuously into the night. I walk for hours—just me, the moon, and the desert—wrapped in layer upon layer of silence. It's almost midnight when I see a small meadow ahead with four tents scattered about. I want to keep hiking but still don't feel brave enough to camp alone, so before reaching the meadow I pull out my sleeping bag, tiptoe over, and settle in. I lie on the earth, gazing at the broad starry night. Even with a long break this afternoon, I was able to knock off 24 miles today, thanks to gentle terrain and night miles. The moon is incredibly bright. I place my open umbrella near my head and scooch under, letting it shield moonlight from my eyes, and help keep night creatures away.

Throughout my journey, I do a lot of night hiking, especially in Northern California and Oregon, and to my surprise, I grow to adore it. It truly works for me. It matches my biorhythm. I learn that I hike best, strong and fast, between the hours of 5 and 10 p.m. If it weren't for the sleeping issues I was having during these early miles on the trail, I doubt I would have ever tried it.

April 26

Morning comes quickly. The other hikers pack up and are gone by five. I rest a bit longer and am walking by 6:30. The trail continues much as it did last night, twisting and turning on dry canyon floors and winding up and down gentle slopes. The cool morning air is lovely. After six miles, I meet a man sitting beside a large white tent stocked with hiker supplies for sale. He offers me a free solar shower. It's an unexpected desert oasis! I take a warm shower, spend a few dollars, and get back on the trail feeling refreshed;

then walk nine miles to Scissors Crossing. There's a large green metal cooler filled with pies, placed here by a "Trail Angel." Who are these Trail Angels and why do they do this? Why are they so helpful to hikers? On top of the cooler is a notebook with a request to sign in and jot down a few thoughts about how things are going. Will there be Trail Angels every few miles, all the way to Canada?

The answer to that question is: No. But in Southern California, where many people are aware of the trail, there are frequent encounters with Trail Angels. So frequent, in fact, that it's easy to hope—even worse—to expect, some sort of delicious surprise to be waiting at every major trail/road intersection. And of course, this doesn't happen. Though for the first few hundred miles, trail magic appears with surprising frequency, and then becomes sparse, until it disappears altogether, and I have to rely only on myself. I'm deeply grateful for the unexpected support in those early miles. It sure was a sweet way to ease into self-reliance.

At Scissors Crossing, I eat a slice of boysenberry pie, then cross the highway and walk until I see a cottonwood tree, which in the afternoon heat looks too good to pass by. I get comfortable under the tall shady tree, though there are snake holes pocking the earth, so I don't relax enough to sleep. I wait out the heat and then hike into the gorgeous San Felipe hills, stopping a few hours later to camp on the edge of a ridge with a thru-hiker whose trail name is Mistletoe. I walked with him earlier today. He's a soft-spoken guy with an advanced degree from Caltech and up until last year was top-dog at a large power plant in Tennessee. He left his job to hike the Appalachian Trail (AT), met the love of his life (at age 62), got married, and bought a small farm in Oregon where he raises goats, has a huge garden, and says he's never been happier.

A fierce wind is blowing and it's tough to put up my tent, but with Mistletoe's help we get it done. I take off the fly (outer layer of tent) because it makes such a racket whipping around in the wind, and then sit inside my tent. For the second night in a row, I watch as the giant yellow moon rises up off the edge of the earth. A feeling of joy sweeps over me. My east coast life slips further and further away as the stars emerge, dotting the purple sky.

April 27

Mistletoe packed up at the crack of dawn and is long gone. I've begun to notice that former ATers (there are many here) tend to hit the trail early. What do they know that I don't? The morning air is moist with pinkish-purple clouds stretched out overhead. As I walk, a double rainbow appears, connecting the brown hills on either side of the valley. After a few hours I come to a water cache where dozens of empty plastic jugs are strung together with rope to keep them from blowing away. A dozen other jugs are full of water, and I replenish my water bottle. I only have 27 miles to go before getting my new sleeping bag. This thought gives me a surge of energy. I quickly get back on the trail, pick up the pace and walk without stopping for the next 11 miles. I skip my afternoon break because the sooner I get to my new gear, the better. I meet two Trail Angels, a husband and wife team, who offer me hot dogs, beer, and cookies. I decline their kind offer and keep moving.

At San Ysidero Creek, I prepare to spend my first night alone. The rain gently taps on the sides of my tent, and when it gets dark all kinds of living, breathing, scampering night creatures come to life. With only a thin piece of fabric separating me from them, my imagination gets carried away. There's a loud thud and I bolt upright! What's that? It grunts and snuffles around. Who's out there? It gets quiet again. When I'm convinced that whatever it

is isn't going to rip my tent apart and devour me, I lie back down
and wait out what I hope is my final cold, uncomfortable, sleepless
night on this long trek north to Canada.

Eagle Rock

April 28

At first light, I walk through an emerald green field covered with
thousands of orange poppies. Looming ahead is a huge natural
rock formation, called Eagle Rock. I stop to have breakfast with
the enormous stone bird, whose wings are spread wide but will
never take flight, and a few miles later arrive in Warner Springs.
Arriving here, at Mile 110, feels like a significant accomplishment.
By 10 o'clock, I've checked into a lovely room and have a whole day
of no hiking ahead of me. Instead I have (what I soon learn will

be) all the usual things a thru-hiker must do when in civilization: do my laundry, eat a big meal, figure out food strategies for the next section of trail, study maps. But before I do any of that, I race over to the post office and pick up my new (borrowed) bag, insulated mat and just in case that isn't enough, a silk sleeping bag liner. Hallelujah! I am so done with being cold at night! *Soooo* done with not sleeping!

April 29 – May 2
At Warmer Springs, I fuel my body with fresh fruits and vegetables and soak my muscles in the enticing hot springs. Once back on the trail, the days pass—extraordinary days filled with bright air, magnificent views, and interesting people. Each day is consumed with walking, one step after another, hour after hour, mile after mile, day after day after day. With each that step I take, I fall more deeply in love with the landscape, more deeply in love with the surprise of each new day, and more deeply in love with life itself. I feel released from my city life. These days in the desert are wide, full, and thrilling. I feel completely at home here, not without concerns, but completely at home in body and spirit. It feels right to be here. It feels right to be doing this.

My new sleep system works like a dream, better than a dream—it's real! I sleep incredibly well and warm. The new insulated air mattress is three inches thick and weighs 1.5 lbs, which is an indulgence since my goal is to travel as light as possible, but it's worth every ounce because it allows me to sleep in comfort wherever I put it. Granite or grass, it doesn't matter. This is my third mat and fourth sleeping bag since I started backpacking 18 months ago, but I've finally got it right! Each night I luxuriate in comfort and warmth, and love the borrowed bag so much that as soon as I can get to a store, I'll buy one.

May 3

I'm walking along the spine of the San Jacinto Mountains and can see forever in every direction! To the east, a faraway black mountain range runs parallel to the one I'm on, other than that everything is light brown and table-flat. Eventually the dry rocky trail turns damp and a few miles later, it's covered with snow. I stop to mix an electrolyte drink, carefully placing my bright blue titanium cup on a boulder. I fill it with water then accidentally knock it and watch as it bounces down the steep cliff. It's a goner. I can't possibly retrieve it without risking life and limb. Drat! I paid full price for that cup (40 bucks). I continue walking on snow until it returns to dry trail, then round a corner and stretched out before me on the path is a hiker taking a nap! He occupies almost the entire trail, but I manage to squeeze by without disturbing him.

Three miles later, I'm on a snowy ridge and lose the trail. I'm not sure where to go next. Footprints lead off in every direction. I pick a random set of tracks to follow and they bring me right back to where I started. Three other hikers arrive on the scene. James and Green Thumb are two guys in their late 20's who are experienced hikers; Carly is a happy, hearty, novice and recent college grad, who took a map and compass course a month ago. They're just as bewildered as me. We find a rock to sit on and try to figure things out. My navigational skills are limited. I don't say much while each of them offers a lengthy theory on which way we should go. Whenever anyone speaks we all listen politely, nod in agreement, and give whatever has just been suggested a try. Several theories later we're still trapped in the snowy quagmire. Just when we've run out of ideas, a thru-hiker returning from Idyllwild, which is where we want to go, shows up and points us in the right direction. It's impossible not to think about the Sierras. If we're baffled by this small patch of snow, what will it be like to navigate through hundreds of miles of the stuff? Will it be like this—walking in circles going nowhere? The only ace in my pocket is that years ago, I spent several summers living and working in the Sierras, plus I've hiked the 215-mile John Muir Trail, a large portion of which is shared with the PCT. Though I failed this snowy test, hopefully in a more familiar landscape I'll succeed.

The four of us walk single file across a snowfield. I hear loud water rushing, but see none in sight. James is walking in front of me when his left leg sinks up to his hip in the snow. (In hiker vernacular this is called post-holing.) He pulls his leg out and we peer down the hole, shocked to see wild, fast-moving water. Where did that come from? Its velocity and depth is astonishing. Now that we know what's beneath us, each step is taken with great care. We make it across the snowfield, find the trail and head down to the trailhead parking lot. Someone offers us a ride into the small mountain village of Idyllwild. According to the sign, it has a population of 3,874 and the elevation is 8,000 feet. We get a site at the campground, which is just a few minutes walk from town.

May 4

I have breakfast with eight other PCTers at a little café. There's joy in the air! We're thrilled to be in town, thrilled to be eating great food, and thrilled to be making progress! We're at mile 178! From my window seat I notice a banner on the front porch of the Idyllwild Inn. It reads: "PCT Hikers Welcome." After a double helping of blueberry pancakes, I register for a room and wander around town waiting for it to become available. Idyllwild is the perfect trail town. It's compact and has everything a thru-hiker could possibly want: post office, laundry, food co-op, and great restaurants. Because the town is small and we're less than 200 miles into this journey, I see lots of other hikers. In a few weeks hikers will drop off the trail in droves due to injury, or for other reasons, but for now we're a plentiful and jubilant bunch. I'm beginning to understand the concept of trail community, which is something I hadn't expected or experienced on my other hikes.

Last year when I thru-hiked the 485-mile Colorado Trail (my longest trail to date) I met only a handful of hikers and spent most of my time alone on that remote, rugged trail, frequently struggling to adapt to the isolation, and assumed the same thing would be true on the PCT. I had no idea that trail community is a normal part of walking a long trail like the PCT or the AT, and I'm surprised to feel part of it. I want to "walk my own walk," at my own pace, any time day or night. I want to take breaks whenever I please and pick campsites that appeal to me, usually high and dry (waterless) sites with wide views. I want to be moved and motivated by what's relevant to my experience, therefore I often walk alone. But I'm also in a flow with several dozen thru-hikers, sometimes walking with them, sometimes camping with them. I usually know who's ahead of me and who is a few miles back. Trail towns are turning out to be a great place to check in, compare notes, and deepen our sense of community.

In contrast, by the time I reach the state of Washington, this trail community dwindles down so much that during the final 500 miles of the PCT, I see only five other northbound PCTers: two couples and one solo hiker. I walk with each of them for just a few miles. But it doesn't much matter, because by then I'm a different kind of hiker; by then I'm a different kind of person.

My room at the Idyllwild Inn is perfect. It's nicely decorated, has a comfortable bed with soft sheets, and a spotless bathroom. By late afternoon, my chores are done and I've mapped out the next 87 miles to Big Bear City. Now it's time to relax. I draw a hot bath, add lavender bath salts, and light a candle—both purchased at the food co-op today. I ease myself into the tub, grab a facecloth, and scrub every inch of my body, then drain out the dirty brown water, and fill up the tub again. I add more lavender salt, lean back, and watch the flickering light. I'm grateful to be here, and grateful for the lifetime of reasons that got me to the trail. Will I make it all the way to Canada? Who knows? I still have more than 2,400 miles to go and that's a long way to walk! I've got many concerns about the hike, but in this moment, with my body submerged in warm sweet-smelling water, I choose to let go of them. For now, all feels right with the world. I linger, then lift my soggy self out of the tub, towel off, and flop on the bed for just a moment. I'll rest for just a minute and then go have dinner. My tired body drifts into a heavy sleep and I never wake, not even once, until morning.

When I open my eyes my entire body is flooded with excitement. What will this new day bring? I can't remember the last time I felt this happy for this long. Each day since starting the trail, I wake with an eager, curious heart. This morning I also happen to be well rested and deeply relaxed, which makes everything seem even more perfect! I reach for my cell phone and turn it on. There's a message from my sister asking me to call. When she answers she says, "Annie, Mom died yesterday."

Suddenly everything shifts. Nothing seems right or reasonable anymore. *Why am I here? What am I doing here?* I pull myself together and step outside. The cute little mountain town that I found so enchanting yesterday feels cold and impersonal today. My hiker friends no longer feel like newfound soul mates but like complete strangers. They, and this town, don't know me. They never met my mother. They don't know that she loves morning glories or can whistle birdcalls or for the past year has been unable to remember my name. They don't know how much I love her. They know nothing.

Cremation papers are faxed to me from 3,000 miles away. In the state of Massachusetts, each child of a deceased parent must sign a form authorizing cremation before the act can be performed. As I hand the papers to the woman on the other side of the counter to fax back to Cape Cod, something inside of me unexpectedly breaks and unstoppable tears stream down my face. She looks up at me, stares for a moment, then hands me my receipt and in a sing-songy voice chirps "Have a nice day!" I turn and walk numbly out the door.

Mom's service will be in 22 days, on the Thursday before Memorial Day. There seems no reason to go home. She's gone. My father passed years ago and my siblings live near one another. It seems to make sense to walk for another 20 days and then go home. Everything feels surreal. I have no evidence that she has died except for a fax indicating that she left yesterday, while I was taking my bath

I came into this world floating naked in the warmth of her body-water. As she leaves—evaporates—I float in the warmth of scented water,

*lavender, like the sachet in her bureau tucked among her nighties.
mother-daughter-sister-water-stranger-friend She! arranged it:
water water water. She! arranged for this familiar room, in this
unfamiliar place. A few nights ago, spread out on the desert floor
between two red boulders, I slept under a fiery sky, and She! came
to me in a dream. She! was translucent—a ghost—hovering above—
swishing this way and that with pearls the size of biscuits 'round her
neck—She! whispered Annie... Annie... I've come to say good-bye.
Is that you mama? Is that really you? Yes, yes, yes, of course, yes! She!
not yet knowing the vacant tongue of death. She! still here, has come
to say good-bye—to spin cartwheels in the creek—to dance the limbo
under prickly arms—She! has come to instruct the desert on how best
to ease my grief—She!—me!—She! THIS! is what the shock of death
does to the living. It releases one from ordinary thought.*

After sending the papers home I walk up the hill to the mountain
shop and buy a new titanium cup and a pair of socks. I feel detached
from my body as if, now, I'm the translucent ghost hovering above.
I leave the store and see a man I know on the other side of the
street. I met him at the kickoff and we've spoken a few times since.
He's about my age and I like him. I cross the road and say hello. We
stand face to face. "I need to talk to someone my own age. Can I
talk to you?" He nods. I look him in the eye and say, "My mother
died yesterday. I found out this morning." Without skipping a beat
he wraps his arms around me. When I look up, he has tears in eyes.
Instinct has drawn me to the right person.

When I arrive back at the inn, some hikers are sitting on the
porch celebrating Cinco de Mayo. Someone hands me a beer. I

can't speak. I don't know how to refuse. I go to my room clutching the cold Dos Equis, and pour it down the sink. Somehow the day passes. She died on May 4th but for me her death day will always be today, May 5th. I spend another night at the inn and a snorer checks into the room next door. His bed is pressed against the thin wall head-to-head with mine. I can't sleep. I take a pillow and blanket and lie on the floor by the bathroom. It's uncomfortable but I stay there all night, not sleeping. The next morning, the innkeeper offers hikers a ride to the trail and I make a snap decision to join them. The only available Internet is at the coffee shop. I run over and hurriedly book a flight then rush back to my room and begin stuffing things into my pack. I ask the innkeeper to wait just a minute and then just one more. I feel pressured and sad and awkward and drained and like I'm holding everyone up, all the while grief lives in me like a trembling secret. I toss my gear into the jeep, hop into the back seat, and we drive off. I can't wait to be alone. I want the desert. I want to move my body and walk. I want to be alone in the desert.

Yesterday at the PCT office we were told that conditions on Fuller Ridge are treacherous. "It's snowy, icy, and dangerous. Someone dies up there every year." They advised us to take an alternate route. I have no problem with that. The innkeeper drops us off at the recommended location, a dirt road that will eventually link up with the trail. I walk with two guys who I've hiked with before and like a lot. Both of them are in their late twenties and are extremely experienced in the wilderness. Miles is tall and thin with shoulder-length dark hair and a steady smile. Gravy is about my height (5' 7"), has short blonde curly hair, piercing blue eyes, and the lightest pack I've ever seen. They're easy-going, strong, smart, and fun. I want to be alone, but for now it feels okay to be with them. After a few miles we hit snow and lose the trail. Once again, I find myself wondering what it will be like to hike in the snowy Sierras. We find the trail, hike out of the snow, and continue along a high ridge. The long flat desert is below, with a highway that cuts right through it. I have cell reception (rare) and stop to call home. I say good-bye to my friends and talk on the phone for quite a while.

When I start hiking again, it's rough going. I push my way through overgrown sections of thorny vegetation that scratch my legs and arms. I see many lizards and a few snakes, all of which make me jump and screech. I'm still not used to reptiles. It's unbearably hot. The trail clings to the side of a rocky canyon wall, the heat radiates off of it and onto me. My damp shirt sticks to my sweaty body. At 2:00 I climb onto a rock, take a few pictures, eat lunch and then continue walking. The hiking is awful. The trail weaves in and out along the canyon wall. I watch my footing closely because I don't want to twist an ankle or fall off the side of the cliff. After several hours of difficult hiking I realize I've left my camera on the rock where I had lunch. The thought of backtracking up this tedious section of trail has zero appeal. I don't go back for it.

The trail begins to descend and I see the highway in the distance. It's a relief to see it, knowing that in just a few hours this unpleasant day will over. I turn a corner and glance ahead noting that the trail hooks a tight turn into a narrow canyon. The canyon is filled with a low cloud, or mist, that's floating up toward me. A quarter-mile later, I turn another bend and suddenly there's fire! That wasn't mist I saw earlier. It was smoke! I can smell it now! Flames are everywhere. I consider turning around but where would I go? The trail behind me is steep and nasty and a day away from Idyllwild. My original plan was to camp six miles from here on the other side of the highway. I stand frozen in place watching the fire and considering the best course of action. I'm not sure how much fire I'll have to walk through, but if I go fast and always have a place of safety in sight, I should be fine. The vegetation is low to the ground; no tall trees will ignite and fall on me. I start walking and see a rock to scramble up onto if need be, and then come to a small stream, which is the first water source today. After filling my bottle, I scan ahead for my next point of safety: a large patch of dirt to the right of the trail about 30 feet away. When I reach it, I see another large rock and cautiously navigate towards it.

After ten minutes of this, I hear shouts: *"Anne! Anne! Come over here!"* It's Miles and Gravy. I run over to them, while carefully avoiding burning grass. We stand together on a large outcropping of rocks. They had stopped to cook an early dinner. It was windy and a flame from Miles' stove ignited a blade of dry grass, touching off the fire. They called 911 and were instructed to find a safe spot to wait for a helicopter and to not let anyone pass through the fire. We wait, not saying much, until the helicopter arrives. It circles above a few times before swooping down and landing with astonishing precision on a nearby boulder. We run over, hop up and climb in. The helicopter lifts, hesitates, then turns and flies out of the canyon. We're only in the air a short time before landing on the median strip in the middle of the busy highway. Officials are waiting for us. They ask a lot of questions, request identification and take our pictures. As we speak with them, plumes of black smoke curl up from behind the hills. Eventually, we're told that we can leave. It will be dark soon and we're not sure where the trail is, but once given permission, we walk away hastily and don't stop until the night is pitch black. We can't find the trail, so we call it a day in an odd spot not far from the highway. We drop our sleeping bags on the ground, a campsite by default, not design. We'll find the trail in the morning.

I crawl into my sleeping bag surrounded by sagebrush and thorny bushes. The highway with its speeding cars is on my left roughly 25 yards away. To my right and much closer are train tracks. Trains pass nearly nonstop, and as each one approaches it blows an angry ear-piercing whistle. The earth shakes and rumbles as they thunder by, leaving an echo of energy reverberating in my bones. It's going to be another long sleepless night.

From our awkward camp, we watch the fire burning the hills, and the headlamps of the fire crew working to put it out. Miles, with his long dark hair and scruffy hiker-beard, holds his head in his hands as he sits atop his sleeping bag. He's beside himself with remorse and anxiety and utterly horrified that a flame from his homemade alcohol stove was the source of such destruction. He's miserable and can't sleep. I try to console him but nothing helps and in a stressful moment he turns to me with his head hung low and an edge in his voice and says, "What's up with you anyway? You won't even tell us what's going on with you!" I'm shocked to hear him say this. I didn't think it showed. "My mother died two days ago. I found out yesterday." Silence. His tone changes and he says he's very sorry; then he gets up and begins to pace. A little later I hear him talking to his parents on his cell phone, first his dad, then his mom. Stretched out on the harsh desert floor, I think about how lucky he is to have the kind of parents he can call at a time like this. I think how lucky he is to have parents at all.

I turn onto my side and look up at the green sign spanning the width of the eastbound lane. Its silver letters read "Desert Towns." Those two words, this dry earth, the thundering trains, the whizzing cars, these two strangers I'm with—all of it makes me feel distant from myself, distant from everything and everyone

I've ever known. I want to sleep but can't. I think about the fire and about my friend's distress. I watch the stars—*and think of her—think of her—think of her—think of her—mama?—I'm falling. I can't stop falling. I fall until sleep catches me.*

It was both a blessing and curse that she died while I was on the PCT. A curse because I wasn't with her, and a blessing because now that I'm back on the trail, I have the desert to escort me into the process of grief. Wild desert-beauty surrounds me by day, and after that first awful night by the highway, empty desert-silence caresses me each night. Each day I wake to a blazing sun that forces me to get up and walk. The desert forces me to keep going. I feel her loss and her presence in everything. When a great blue heron flies before me, a bird not normally seen in this desert environment, I know in my heart that it's her. I fix my eyes on her prehistoric profile and watch as she drifts across the sky. When my eye catches tiny bright blue flowers staring up at me from the desert sand, they remind me of her, and at night when I sleep, she continues to visit my dreams. I can think of no better way of soothing the raw sadness that lives in me than by being here, in this mystical, magical place.

May 7

We're up at the crack of dawn and easily find the trail. A few miles later we come to a small building located on the Mesa Wind Farm. Two employees invite us in to fill our water bottles. One of them points to a freezer where ice cream is sold. I splash water on my face in the ladies room and then purchase an Eskimo Pie. A hiker from Japan named Sushi joins us. He's in his thirties and speaks very little English. Instead of talking he smiles a lot with his bright engaging eyes. What's it like for him hiking this long trail in a foreign country? I see him on and off for the next thousand miles, during which time his English improves a great deal.

Miles is worn out from the stress of the fire and decides to drop off the trail. Convincing him to stay is useless. Gravy remains with him while he figures out logistics. I get back on the trail. It's stifling hot as I climb 2,000 feet to the arid ridge behind the wind farm. When I reach the top, the trail dips down slightly but mostly stays high for the rest of the morning. The day grows increasingly hot. Because of the heat, it's hard to walk, hard to breathe. I'm especially grateful to have my reflective umbrella to help shield the penetrating rays of sun. I meet a young hatless guy from Georgia, named Little Brother, sitting in the sun. His skin is bright red and his clothes are soaked with sweat. He looks like he's just jumped out of a lake, but there's no water up here. He tells me that he's tired and needs a break. We say good-bye and as I turn to leave, I almost step on a big fat snake.

It's silent and surprisingly gorgeous in these rough, stark hills, located in the San Gorgonio Wilderness. This empty landscape captivates me in a way I never thought possible. I never thought I could like such a place but I do, except for the relentless heat, which makes everything hard. When I come to the next junction, I leave the trail and hike to Whitewater Preserve to wait out the afternoon heat.

The preserve is lovely, replete with a small visitor center, natural history displays, and a big, clean restroom. After cooling off inside, I walk to a buggy field, pitch my tent in the shade and read the hot afternoon away. I meet two hikers who are planning to spend the night here, and before I leave we all take a swim in the "natural" manmade pond. I walk alongside Whitewater Creek for six miles and then need to cross it. This task requires some thought because it's the first real creek crossing I've encountered, and the wide water is running fast. I stumble around on river rocks searching for the best place to cross and come upon on the biggest, fattest, most colorful snake I've ever seen in the wild. Uck! It has yellow, black, and red rings around its slimy body. Snakes! I almost didn't attempt this hike because of my fear of snakes. At home I did everything I could to prepare myself for them. Knowledge is power: I read books. I watched documentaries. When I was in DC last month I went to the reptile hut at the National Zoo and in that smelly muggy place, I watched as an anaconda coiled itself up and pressed against the giant glass window mere inches from my nose. It was then that I thought, "Ok fine, if I can stand this close to that monster I must be cured."

But I'm not. The multi-colored snake in front of me now creeps me out in a big way. All logic suggests it's just a harmless, sleepy 'ole snake, but I freak out anyway. I run away from it and kick into a primordial state of snake hyper-alert. I quickly find a decent place to ford the creek and scuttle across. Once on the other side, there's a flat spot that would make an ideal camp. It's 6 p.m. and I've only hiked 12 miles today. I feel pressured to keep going as there's still plenty of daylight, plus it's starting to cool off, but I'm exhausted. I've slept very little the past two nights. An image of the fat snake slithering around on the other side the creek comes to mind. Does he like to swim? Does he have relatives living on this side of the creek? I set up my tent and once inside still don't feel protected. I imagine snakes crawling all over me while I sleep. And that's when *I snap!*

I can't do this any more! This irrational fear of snakes has got to go! It's too stressful and consumes too much of my mental energy. I can't continue like this. I need to look at things differently. I need

Desert Camp

to make friends with the enemy. I hatch a plan: I'll befriend them by naming each snake, like hurricanes. Instead of screaming each time I see one of those slimy, fork-tongued, creepy crawlers, I'll bestow the name of a female friend, niece, or sister upon it. I've seen eight snakes so far. The ninth letter of the alphabet is "I." I'll christen my next snake Isis Ina Isabella. There, I feel better. I have a plan.

I eat three rice cakes smeared with peanut butter and sip tea from my new silver titanium cup. I watch as the sun sets and all is cast in a wash of orange-pink-purple light: the muddy earth, the polished rocks, the waist-high bushes, even my skin is tainted a purplish hue. Darkness descends and a few stars come forth, then hundreds appear, then thousands. I lay on my back watching the night, listening to the creek, and waiting for sleep.

Mama? Mama, can you hear me?
Mama? Mama, can you see me?

2

Whitewater Creek to Forester

Walk as if you are kissing the earth with your feet.
~ THICH NHAT HANH

May 8
5:30 a.m.

The heat trapped inside my tent behaves like a cat slinking around inside a small cage. It pushes up against my legs, nestles itself on my lap, then crawls onto my chest, kneading its bumpy little paws on my face until I can no longer sleep. I wake covered in sweat, kick off my bag, unzip the tent and let the annoying animal out the door. Oh, such heat! I quickly pack up, get on the trail and walk a few miles to Mission Creek, where I splash water on my face, and make coffee.

When it's time to leave I rock-hop across the creek, proud of myself for having kept my shoes dry. A few minutes later, the trail crosses the creek again, then again, and again. I check the map and note that the trail crisscrosses at least a dozen more times, so I forget about dry shoes, and for the next 15 miles slosh my way through water. I walk slightly uphill all day under a blazing sun with distant mountains ahead and a multitude of lizards flouncing at my feet. They scurry in front of me, strike a pose, then dart into the bushes. One funny-looking creature about eight inches tall, stands on his hind legs, then races up the trail in front of me. He looks like a miniature dinosaur and is so enthralling that I forget for a moment that I don't much care for reptiles and race after him. I want to get a closer look at this magnificent creature and chase him until he slips between two boulders and is gone.

Last night I made a conscious decision to befriend snakes and today I'm chasing lizards? What's going on? I've only hiked 225 miles. What will I be chasing in another 2,000 miles? Grizzlies? The natural world seems to be pulling me deeper and deeper into itself, allowing me—a stranger, a city girl—to see, feel and be with its beastly, earthly, and temporal dimensions in ways that I never knew possible. Without the distractions of city life, the earth's subtle pulse is a faintly perceptible rhythm to which I now walk. Every cell in my body is lulled by its beat, as I ease myself into each new day, and traipse through this otherworld.

In the afternoon I meet two thru-hikers taking a break in the shade. Derek and Crackers saw the note I posted at Mesa Wind Farm regarding my lost camera. "Good news" Crackers says, "An old guy named Appleface found it and he's only a few miles back." Crackers is in his twenties, has long black flowing hair, lives in New York City, and is wearing a red plaid kilt. "Heck, he's been carrying the extra weight of your camera for miles. You should go get it." Apparently even the effects of a mild Catholic upbringing still live in me somewhere because upon hearing this, I'm instantly consumed with guilt. Yikes, I'm burdening someone with the weight of my 3-oz camera? I must go rescue him. I drop my pack and run down the trail in search of him.

It feels glorious to move my body without a 30-lb pack strapped to my back! The runner that I am takes over as I jog downhill.

What sweet relief it is to run! What sweet relief it is to stop being a backpacker and be who I truly am! After two miles, I've still not seen any sign of Appleface. I give up the search and run back, retrieve my pack, and begin the steep climb up to a forested ridge.

The light softens as the sun slips behind a dense mass of fir trees. I pass Derek camped alone in a cozy little spot by the side of the trail and give him some valerian, an herb known for its relaxing qualities, because he says he hasn't been sleeping well. He's a clean-cut guy in his thirties and very nice. As we're chatting, Crackers comes running up the trail waving his arms wildly and shouting that he's just seen a huge bear. I'm shocked by this news because bears are not at all on my mind. I thought I had until at least the Sierras before I needed to be bear-aware. Though, come to think of it, we are heading to Big Bear City.

Because of this news, I'm tempted to stay with them but instead hike another hour and make camp at 8,000 feet, surrounded by snow. It's very cold. Did I really wake up to oppressive heat this morning? I pitch my tent near a guy named TK (short for Too Kool,) and once inside I again consider the bear. All those years of living in Yosemite (decades ago) have brain-washed me into believing that even so much as *thinking* about food while in a tent, is enough to provoke a bear into doing dangerous things. I'll pick up my bear canister, which is required in national parks, before entering the Sierras at Mile 702, but for now, here I sit at Mile 235 with a stinky food bag. I wonder if I should tell TK about the bear sighting? On my way to stash my food bag under a pile of rocks, far from my tent, I decide to warn him and crouch down next to his tent door. As we speak, I notice he's using what looks like his food sack for a pillow. I prattle on about the bear and about how the kilt guy said it was a huge one and about how I thought he might want to know "in case you have any food in your tent." He nods politely, and as I plop rock after rock after rock atop my food bag, his light goes out and he begins to snore.

May 9
It's a cold morning. I can see my breath as I walk from my high camp toward Onyx Summit, at 8,600 feet. At home I live 19 feet above sea level. I huff and puff, still adjusting to elevation. There are a few steep, icy sections that require my full attention. After a dozen miles the trail descends, merging with a dirt road, and things get much easier. I follow the road until mid-afternoon, passing a mansion along the way with a lion, tiger, elephant and leopard roaming in the yard. Later someone tells me that an animal trainer for the movie industry lives there.

I come to a red velvet sofa placed under a few scraggily trees and a sign welcoming hikers. There are two red coolers filled with apples, oranges, sodas and cookies. Taped onto one of the coolers are phone numbers of places to stay in Big Bear City (population 12,000) and I jot them down. After a short break, I walk until the woods give way to endless fields of tall brown grass. A fierce wind kicks in, blowing across the open land and directly into my face. It's exhausting pushing my way through the firm wind, which I do for many hours before arriving at Hwy 18. The highway is an empty, two-lane road. I wait a long time for a ride and when I finally arrive in town, I get a private room at the youth hostel and then treat myself to french fries and salad at a nearby restaurant. Today was my longest day so far: 24 miles. It's Mother's Day.

May 10
I track down Appleface. The "old guy" is at least ten years my

junior, probably in his early forties. I try to give him 20 bucks for carrying my camera 70 miles but he refuses by saying "just buy me a beer sometime." He tells me that whenever he took a picture with his camera, he also took one with mine and he hopes I don't mind. Mind? Why would I mind? Now, not only do I have my camera back, I also have pictures from that piece of trail! Sweet! While waiting for the bus back to the hostel, I look at his pictures. It seems he favors two subjects: delicate wildflowers and drinking beer with his buddies.

May 11 – 13

In Big Bear City I attempt to sate an insatiable appetite. I've always been passionate about food but these days I obsess over it. If I'm not eating, I'm thinking about eating. At the grocery store I fine-tune my selections for the next section of trail and am determined to have enough with me this time. I always run out. The first two days after a re-supply are great! I often start out with an avocado, orange, apple, carrots, chocolate, couscous, cheese, pita, and something salty, like corn nuts. After all that's eaten, I scrape by on trail bars and dried fruit. I usually run out of food the day before coming into town. For this next 98-mile section to Wrightwood, I'm determined to get it *Wright!* I want to carry enough nutritious food with me so that I don't run out.

I get a ride to the trail and begin walking beneath a cloudless sky that's as wide and as blue as the sea. I meander along the edge of a forest with panoramic views of Big Bear ski area; the trail then twists and turns inward through a forest. Later, I arrive at a huge burn area, the result of a forest fire, and am stunned. It's shocking to see hundreds of thin, scorched trees coated with a thick, burnt crust. Some have toppled over but most remain upright, appearing like bony relics of their former selves. I imagine their hollow dead eyes watching me, as I briskly glide through their graveyard. I've never seen a burn area this vast, and find it disturbing. I fail to see beauty or hope in this place, and am unnerved by what feels like a landscape beholden to grief. A part of me knows that tucked away inside this scorched mess exists the potential for new growth, new plants, new life. There's sure to be renewal in this dismal place. Someday it will flourish again, but in this moment, stepping on ashy earth, I can't imagine it. I see and smell only the remains of a forest bereft of its former life. I spend several hours walking in the burnt woods. When the lush green forest returns, the taste of smoke in my mouth and irritation in my eyes begins to abate.

At sunset, I camp with ten others at Bear Creek. I walked 20 miles today.

May 14

It's a moonless night and I'm standing on a cliff high above a wide, rambunctious creek. It's long past time to quit walking for the day. I've been searching for a good campsite but nothing pleases me. Every possible spot is much too steep. It's almost 11:00 and I'm tired of searching. I give up and call the tilted brittle earth at my feet home for the night. Once settled, I place my pack under the right side of my sleeping mat, which helps keep me level, and then gaze through the mesh at tens of thousands of bright blinking stars.

There's no wind tonight. All is still. I hear the faint sound of the creek, but mostly what I hear is silence. Deep silence. I hear it crawling around outside my tent and scratching up against trees. I feel it roaming freely through the chambers of my heart and pumping through my veins. The quiet, and stillness, make me uneasy. I feel skittish and very alone. I try to relax, reminding myself that this is why I came here—to walk on the earth, to sleep on the earth, to listen to the earth's silence, and to feel uneasy. *I came here to feel uneasy.* I came here of my own volition, to live for a time in this natural world. Since there's no other choice, I kiss the ache of loneliness and the quiver of fear goodnight, and turn again to admire the infinite stars above. My companions.

23 miles.

May 15

At sunrise, I cross Deep Creek Bridge. On the other side, the trail is carved into soft, rust-colored rock. The texture and color mesmerize me, until I turn a corner and the captivating red rock is sprayed black with graffiti. I'm less than 100 miles from L.A.— city-art meets desert rock. After a few miles, I arrive at a parking lot, lose the trail, and walk into a dry basin via a maze of dusty jeep roads. I head for a paved road on the horizon, along the way passing a large green canvas tent with a row of empty whiskey bottles lined up in front. Who's inside? I keep walking. I splash through a creek, walk a bit further, then meet a Trail Angel sitting on a lawn chair waiting, it seems, just for me.

She gets up to fix me a root beer float. When she hands me the tantalizing potion, I push the lump of vanilla ice cream that's bobbing at the surface, into the bubbly tonic, watching as an icy crust forms, then pick it up with my fingers and crunch my teeth into it. It's 8 a.m. and I'm having a root beer float for breakfast. The Trail Angel is a minister. She wants to hike the PCT someday and is here "to do research." She asks a lot of questions about gear.

After we say good-bye, I walk alongside dry brown hills for many hours and then see something move swiftly across the trail in front me, and into the brush. It must be a snake, my first since vowing to befriend them. Then a strange thing happens: I lean over to get a better look. The odd creature has a lime green head and a bright orange neck. She's exotic! But because she's half hidden I'm not sure if she's a snake or just a lizard? No matter. This is the first time in my life that I've ever leaned over to get a better look at a creature I initially thought was a snake. She deserves a snake name whether she is one or not! I christen her with the name I picked out nine days ago: Isis, Ina, Isabella.

During the next hour I see two more, both of them definitely snakes. The first one, Joy-Jen-Janie-Jude, is three feet long and has yellow stripes on either side of her shiny black back. She is motionless, basking in the afternoon sun, as I sneak by. The next one, a tiny little thing, is only about four inches long and has red, black, and white rings looping down the length of her pencil-thin body. She's a baby and the name I have at-the-ready is Kaelyn. I take a picture, thinking that my two-year old great-niece Kaelyn might like to see a snapshot of her namesake. I mean name-snake.

I consider snakes as I walk and find myself hoping that the next one, the L-snake, will be a rattler. *I'm hoping to see a rattler?* This can't be so! I'm not only hoping to see a snake, which is bizarre, but I'm hoping to see a rattler? Clearly, this little game has gotten out of control.

May 16

It's an intensely hot afternoon. I'm especially grateful to have my umbrella to help shield the sun. It's like walking with my own portable shade tree, plus, this way I don't have to wear a hat. I climb to the top of a tall brown hill and see a train chugging slowly beside the highway below. How long is that train? A mile? Two miles? I watch it chug along as I walk, keeping an eye out for the caboose, but it never arrives. When I reach the highway there's a dark, damp, metal tunnel under it that I'm supposed walk through—that is, if I wish to take advantage of the fast food joint on the other side. I tell myself that going through the unpleasant-looking tunnel is a small price to pay for the pleasure of eating hot, greasy, salty french fries. I take a deep breath and run through it as fast as I can.

When I arrive at Mickie D's, there are six hikers feasting on junk food. I order a salad, french fries, lemonade, and as a special treat, an iced coffee to pour into my water bottle for breakfast tomorrow.

At the convenience store next door, I charge my iPod and cell phone behind a pinball machine and when that's done, walk back to the tunnel. Here we go again. This time I put on my headlamp, take a deep breath, pause, and then go for it! I run through the smelly, damp, dark underpass, and just before reaching the light at the end of the tunnel, a baby rattler appears at my feet! My L-snake is a rattler! I'm momentarily elated that my wish has come true, but then remember that baby rattlers are more dangerous than full-grown ones. I've read they'll strike at anything, even without provocation, because they haven't yet learned to not waste venom on victims they can't possibly consume. Victims, for instance, like me. I leap over it while flailing all four limbs in air, and hit the pavement running. When I'm safely out of the tunnel, I turn around and walk back to take a picture of Laura-Linnie.

I return to the trail, and six miles later spend the night in a campground with three other thru-hikers. We're camped at Mile 350—only 2,300 miles to go.

May 17

Strolling through a nameless little town in the pale morning light,

Laura Linnie

I pass a shooting range where two sad-looking dogs are chained to a stake. They bark and growl, and pull on their chains as I pass. The road is littered with empty bullet shells. There's a strange vibe in the air. I can't wait to get out of here, and walk as fast as I can until I'm back on the trail, climbing toward a high green ridge. Halfway up, I meet a hiker taking a break by a narrow stream. He tells me that in that odd section:

- He saw three men running and hiding in bushes, while a border patrol helicopter flew overhead.
- A thru-hiker left her pack by the road and walked a few yards away to get water. When she returned her pack was gone.
- Someone threw a headless rattlesnake out a car window, aiming it at two hikers.

I spend the rest of the day ridge walking. I should be used to encountering snow when I least expect it, but I'm not. The trail that splits off toward Wrightwood is hidden under a deep layer of the stuff. In order to avoid the snow I walk an extra seven miles on dry trail to an empty road, where I hope to catch a ride. An hour later, the first car approaches and drives by without even a glance. The prospect of walking another six miles into town (after having walked 22 already) is an unpleasant one, but it's better than just sitting here. I get up and start hiking. A hundred yards down the road a dark green Subaru pulls up beside me, and an older woman in the passenger seat rolls down her window. In a loud raspy voice she says, "Honey, would ya like a ride?"

Esther is 75 and her husband Harry, behind the wheel, is 91. Both are sharp as tacks, self-assured, kind, and funny. Esther has plucky, upfront western charm and talks a blue streak. Harry chimes in whenever he can with a pithy comment or two. Esther offers me doughnuts and tells me she was born and bred in Wrightwood and that Harry is her second husband. She says Harry was born in New Bedford, MA. When he finds out I'm from Boston he's tickled pink, and then cautions me: "Don't ever move out here. The politics are *awful!*"

Esther and Harry have a guest cabin on their property and insist that I spend the night. Esther is leaving the next morning on a trip with her girlfriends to Catalina Island. She says that she and Harry often drive up the road looking for hikers. She doesn't say it outright, but I'm pretty certain she came up here tonight specifically looking for someone like me to stay in the cabin and check-in on Harry while she's away. It works out perfectly for all of us. The cabin has it's own kitchenette and bathroom. It's lovely.

I'm ahead of schedule. I only have 125 miles to hike before catching my plane home next week. I either need to slow my pace, or spend a few extra days in Wrightwood. I choose the latter, and stay three nights in the guest cabin. Harry and I have dinner together each night. He tells me stories about when he was a flight squadron leader in WW II during the Battle of the Bulge. He says war is a horrible thing but he didn't realize just how horrible at the time because he was flying his planes high up in the sky, above it all. He shows me black and white photos of a handsome young man in uniform, standing beside a snappy-looking plane.

We talk about his life growing up in New Bedford and we talk about baseball. He's an avid Red Sox fan, and says he can't bear to listen to a game when they're losing. In fact, one night while we're having dinner and listening to a Red Sox game (they're losing) he gets up, stomps over to the radio, and shuts it off. "I can't take it anymore. Those bums!" My father used to say same thing! If my dad were alive, he would be the same age as Harry, and I can't help missing him. He would have liked Harry.

I spend my time in Wrightwood visiting shops, catching up with other hikers, re-supplying, and getting to know Harry quite well. I discover a coffee shop that offers a free cup of Joe to thru-hikers willing to have a picture taken and tacked onto the wall. I grin in front of the lens and watch as my mug shot is taped on the wall beside the clock. A mug for a mug. It's a great cup of coffee, too. It turns out to be one of only four good cups I will have on the entire trail! (The other good coffee is in Idyllwild, CA—mile 178, Drakesbad, CA—mile 1354, and at Timberline Lodge, Oregon—mile 2107)

May 20

Harry graciously offers to drive me back to the trail. As I get out of the car he takes off his navy blue Red Sox cap with the red B, and says, "Here, this is for you. Take a picture of yourself when you get to Canada and send it to me. I know you're going to make it."

I'm touched by both his kind gesture, and his vote of confidence. If Harry—who for years has been sizing up hikers as they pass through Wrightwood—believes in me, then maybe I will make it to Canada. I give him a peck on the cheek and get back on the trail. (Since I don't wear baseball caps, I leave it behind when I fly home. After I finish the trail, I send Harry a photo-shopped picture of me at the Canadian border wearing the cap.)

I waste an hour walking on a mish-mash of deer paths that lead nowhere, then find the trail, and meet two friendly young guys named Weed and Chester. We hike together, moving along at a nice clip toward Mt. Baden Powell. Weed is in front when he lights a joint, takes a drag, and passes it back to his friend. Chester takes a long drag and then to my surprise says, "Here, Anne, you want some?" I wasn't expecting this offer and am completely thrown off. People still smoke that stuff? *Why?* I can't even remember the last time I smelled it. I don't like smoke of any kind, but am relieved that instead of a lecture, I hear myself say, "Ah, no thanks. I'm a runner." Huh?

Mt. Baden Powell is covered with snow. I take the alternate route down a long canyon, reach a campground, and spy a metal picnic table in the shade. I get comfortable on it and take a short nap. Refreshed, I eagerly get back on the steep trail. It weaves through a forest of short, twisted, gnomish-looking trees. Halfway up the ridge, I meet four guys. We leapfrog a few times before they disappear ahead of me. At sunset, we meet again and camp. I beeline over to a picnic table and prepare for the night. Two picnic table beds in one day! What luck! I love to sleep on them because: a) They're level; b) I don't have to bother with a tent; and c) I get to sleep under the stars without worrying about wild things stumbling onto me during the night.

Picnic Table Nap

May 21

I'm walking through acres and acres of Joshua trees just after dawn, when a reddish glow appears on the eastern horizon. Darkness converges with light and a purple blush spills onto the earth, the trees and me. I watch as the red ball of fire lifts itself from the edge of the earth. Good Morning Sunshine!

I walk on the road until reaching the small dusty town of

Littlerock, which has a strong Mexican flair to it, and stop at a restaurant to order beans, rice, and quesadillas for breakfast. When it's time to leave, I'm loathe to step back into the heat, so instead of hiking I poke around in a few stores before seeking out the library, which is located in a one-room cinder block building. I take refuge under the air conditioner, letting its icy breath blow onto my neck while I watch the locals check out books, chat with one another, and stop to read flyers hanging by the thick metal door. Me, a stranger with a backpack, sitting silently, observing this sweet community come and go. Then I get down to the task of writing my mom's eulogy.

When it's my turn to push open the thick metal door, I'm assaulted by ferocious heat. It squeezes my body, making it hard to breathe. I slowly find my way to the road. The trail is closed for the next 50 miles due to fire. Most hikers hate road walks, but I don't mind. It's a change of pace, plus it doesn't bother my feet. I've run thousands of miles on pavement; my feet are used to it. For many hikers, roads mean blisters, blisters, and more blisters. I meet a hiker named Smokey. He introduces me to the woman he's with, her name is Idaho. She's holding a transistor radio the size of a loaf of Wonder Bread, and tells me she listens to AM talk shows as she walks. That evening, I learn she also walks with vodka, and is a Sarah Palin fan. To my complete surprise, we seem to enjoy each other's company.

The three of us camp in a field. In the morning when I hear them stirring, I force myself to get up. We spend the day walking on pavement. At one point, we walk on a narrow piece of road with tight curves and fast cars, which is not very fun. But before we know it we've knocked off 20 miles and arrive at a campground, where we take showers, eat ice cream, and stretch out on soft green grass.

May 22

I don't get up in time to walk with Smokey and Idaho, so walk
19 solo miles to the town of Agua Dulce, where Trail Angels offer
an amazing retreat to hikers. In their gorgeous backyard are six
large white tents with four cots in each. There are also showers,
Internet, and bicycles available if you want to ride into town. Most
amazing to me is that they provide clean clothes to wear while
they do your laundry. They even run the dirty laundry through the
washer twice to get it super-clean before drying!

There's a two-night limit and we (me, Smokey and Idaho)
stay both nights, then walk another 25 easy, happy miles together,
stopping at one point to inspect mountain lion tracks. As we're
examining them, Smokey says, "This has been the best year of my
life." These bold words puzzle me. How can a person commit to
such a statement?

It takes me quite a long time (years, actually) before realizing,
that for me, these months on the trail wrapped in joy, grief,
curiosity, fear, awe, bliss, hunger, connection, isolation, uncertainty,
and astonishment—were some of the best days of my life, too.

May 24

The trip to the Los Angeles airport begins with a harrowing ride
on a busy freeway. In the car with me are two other hikers who are
also leaving the trail. Creaky is in the back seat with me, Memphis
is in front with Shelley, the insane (but kind) woman behind the
wheel. She's a friend of a friend of a friend I met fifteen minutes
before getting into the car. In other words, I have no idea who this
crazed woman squealing around corners and weaving through
rush hour traffic at 90 mph is. Several times we come within
inches of smacking the left side of the car into a concrete divider

and smashing into other cars. I'm surprised and quite pleased to step out of the car alive.

I get to know my fellow travelers over dinner at Denny's. Memphis is going home because of a knee injury. He'd taken to the trail still heartbroken over the death of his only child seven years ago. He was hoping to finish the trail on what would have been his son's 10th birthday.

Creaky says he's going home because he doesn't feel right. He's done the trail before and feels crummy this time and sees no point in continuing. The motel is full, so the three of us share a room. I sleep on the floor. Creaky insists that I take a bed but I insist on the floor. As soon as the lights go out Memphis starts snoring like a champion boxer. All night long, he blissfully heaves and snorts, making sleep for the rest of us impossible. I wait out the night on the concrete floor and am greatly relieved when morning finally arrives. (After returning home, Creaky has a heart attack but recovers just fine.)

May 25 – 29
Cape Cod, Massachusetts
Mom's service is a beautiful, thoughtful, lively, musical, magical, poetic celebration of life. Hers is the loveliest service I've ever attended. (I have my younger sister to thank for that.) There's song and laughter, reflection and love, long walks on the beach, and then, in what feels like no time at all, I find myself on a plane heading west, to a trail that now feels like a long ago faded dream.

May 29, 30
Once I arrive in L.A., I make my way back to Agua Dulce via train and taxi, then re-hike 25 miles of trail. When I walked this section

with Smokey and Idaho, it was a cloudy, cool day. Today it was all about heat. I'm camped near an empty ranger station and am exhausted, jet-lagged, and disoriented. It was awkward to leave the trail, and it's even more awkward to return. I get into my sleeping bag and reach for my wallet. A jolt of adrenalin shoots through my body—I haven't seen it since the taxi ride and frantically search but can't find it. What a hassle it will be if I have to replace my license, credit cards, and ATM card. I empty my pack. I scour every inch of the tent. I look through all my clothes. I'm deeply distressed and keep looking, but it doesn't surface. Out of options, I whisper a prayer to Mom, figuring why not? She may still be lingering between this world and that. I ask her to please help. I'm sick with fatigue and worry but I sleep. In the morning, the wallet is beside my head. Thanks *Mom?* I'm always suspicious when I hear stories like this, but that's what happened.

May 31

I meet a guy named Pretty Good as he's getting dropped off at the trail. He recently returned from a tour of duty in Iraq and after getting released from service he thought it would be relaxing to hike the PCT. I ask him how it's going so far and he says, "Well, pretty good. I just spent two days in the hospital passing a kidney stone and a few more days recovering. Other than that, things are pretty good." The next time I see him, 200 miles up the trail, I ask him how it's going and he says, "Well, pretty good. I got bit by a rattlesnake last week, had hallucinations, and went to the ER to get an anti-venom shot. Other than that, things are pretty good." Then he shows me the fang marks.

I still feel out-of-sorts from the trip home. Instead of walking with Pretty Good, I go into the town of Lake Hughes (population

649) and crash in a small, shady field. It's Memorial Day. I rest, re-group, and try to adjust to being a hiker again. The day melts away. I make my way back to the trail, hike a few miles and camp on sandy earth, watching as the sun sets, shedding iridescent light all over the desert. I'm back. I'm here. I'm in the natural world again, away from cities, away from crowds, away from my mother's ashes.

I only walked 8 miles today.

June 1
Pinecones placed together to form the number 500, are in front of me on the trail. Thru-hiker communication. This is the 500-mile mark, and the longest I've ever hiked on one trail. I make up for my short day yesterday by walking 29 miles today and spend the night camping on the edge of the Mojave Desert.

Pine Cone Mile Market

June 2, 3

I'm three miles into the Mojave and don't feel well. A sour stomach combined with intense heat is making me miserable. I throw up, walk another mile, and throw up again. I seek shelter under a small bush. What about snakes? I feel too crappy to care. As the sun moves, the shade offered by the little bush also moves. Each time the shade leaves, I pick up my ground cloth and follow it. Hours pass. I see a very tall man dressed in white walking briskly up the sandy path. Feeling a little better, I gather my gear and step out to join him. He tells me he's from England and has been walking 25 miles a day since Mexico. He seems to be in a bit of a stupor, but that's normal. Everyone I meet in the Mojave is in a bit of stupor. The wind is blowing hard. We make it to a bridge and I manage to choke down some food, and sip a little water. The wind is incredibly strong. The Englishman has clocked his 25 miles for the day and camps at the bridge. I lean into the wind, walk until well after dark, and camp a half mile from a guy named Socks. These days, if someone is camped within a mile, it feels like I have company!

The next day high tech windmills tower above me like giants with metal blades for arms. I pass hundreds of them and see hundreds more on nearby ridges. I also see a rattler. Normally snakes move off the trail when they feel footstep vibration, but not this rattler, Paula-Paulette. She's used to the hum and shake of windmills and isn't the least bit fazed by my presence. She doesn't budge. I feel like a contemporary Doña Quixote, with my silver umbrella held shield-like in case she gets feisty.

After 17 hot miles, I hitch into the town of Tehachapi and spend two nights.

June 5

I'm camped on the side of a hill with a spectacular view of big sky and endless desert. The wind is fierce. It pushes my tent this way and that, as it blows through the mesh walls. It's no easy thing to sleep under an open umbrella inside a one-person tent, but that's what I do. The umbrella helps keep the wind off my face and sand out of my eyes.

June 6

I never want to see another windmill as long as I live. Windmills represent wind, and constant wind is a difficult companion to befriend.

Tehachapi Pass

June 7

I arrive at a much-needed water cache and take a few ounces (there's not much), under the observant eye of five thru-hikers (whom I don't know) who are sitting under a nearby Joshua tree. I go over and introduce myself, then spend the afternoon with them under the tree, dodging the heat, and sharing trail stories. At 5 p.m., I start walking again. There are scorpions on the path. I hustle by them and four hours later see TK (Too Kool) camped a few yards off-trail. I haven't seen him since that night near Big Bear City when the kilt guy saw a bear. I pitch my tent near his. I'm very thirsty and out of water. Without asking, TK generously offers me some of his water.

June 8

When I wake up, TK is gone. I walk nine miles to the next water cache and it's empty. Not even a drop. I know better than to rely on caches. They're not meant to be primary water sources. They exist because some kind soul has lugged water to a remote location. I think back to yesterday morning when I passed a bubbling creek, and chide myself for not hydrating better. I filled up my water bottles but should have filled up my body too. The dry desert landscape is beginning to merge with the Southern Sierras. Yesterday's vibrant creek made me think that I no longer needed to worry about water. That was a mistake because a few miles later, the waterless desert returned. Now here I am with a parched throat, flat out of water, and flat out of luck.

According to the water report, if I turn left in six miles and walk .7 miles to a meadow, there might be a seep. A seep is exactly what it sounds like: a trickle of water that seeps out of something—a rock, mud, a meadow. If a seep isn't flowing, you can dig around it and sometimes make it flow.

I set my sights on finding the seep but first have a long, tedious climb ahead of me. I swallow two electrolytes capsules and begin. My mood is low. All I can think about is my thirst. I'm crazed with desire for water. I feel lethargic, walking slowly and miserably until reaching the intersection. When I arrive at the meadow, I see water oozing from mud. I dig hungrily, like a puppy in search of a hidden bone, until water begins to flow. I fill two bottles and immediately drink them. Sweet relief! After an hour of resting and hydrating, I come back to life. I hike up the hill to the trail, accidentally leaving behind three pairs of sweaty socks drying in the sun.

The rest of the day is pure joy! The terrain shifts from dry golden desert to moist green mountains and I arrive at Walker Pass clocking my first 30-mile day. The rumor that there might be a Trail Angel at Walker Pass is true! Since there's only half a trail bar in my food bag, I'm elated. Trail Angel Mary has covered a picnic table with bread, cheese, tomatoes, salad, peanut butter, salty chips, pretzels, cookies, wine, beer, soda, oranges, apples and only in California—an entire crate of ripe avocados! We have dinner together, and she tells me she's here for a week helping hikers. She says it gives her an excuse to come to the mountains and meet quirky characters.

In the past four days, I've hiked 12, 25, 25, and 30 miles. This is the first time I've ever walked three 25's in a row and I'm beat. I sleep late the next morning and though I'm eager to get to Kennedy Meadows, the final stop before the Sierras, I decide to rest. I get back on the trail at noon, grateful for the tremendous gift of good food and good company.

June 11

Just before Kennedy Meadows, a wide, gray-green river comes into view—the Kern River—it's the largest body of water I've seen in 700 miles. Hallelujah! Big water! This means I'm out of the desert for sure! I'm out of the constant heat and constant search for water! In the cool Sierras there'll be plenty of clear, delicious H_2O. I'm done with filtering water from stagnant pools! Done with vigilantly checking the water report! Done with walking a mile off-trail to find a seep! No more parched throat, no more sand in my socks, or up my nose! And no more snakes! (I saw a total of 38 snakes in the desert, including 14 rattlers.)

At the Kennedy Meadows General Store, I celebrate my arrival by purchasing an outdoor shower. I wrap the fluffy yellow towel that comes with the fee, around my body, and lean in to turn on the water. The sky darkens, and suddenly a hard, cold rain hammers down onto me. No matter. Who cares? I'm here! I've just spent six weeks walking 702 miles in a hot dry desert. Bring on the rain! Remind me that I've left that enigmatic place, with its cool nights and hot days, its brittle earth and high hills, its spiky critters and metal windmills. Remind me that I've left all that behind! I step into the shower to scrub the last traces of desert from my pores, fully aware that my efforts are in vain. It's too late. The desert has penetrated far beneath the surface of my skin. There's no getting rid of it now. It lives in me, permanently, somewhere close to my heart.

June 12, 13
I tweak my gear for the Sierras by adding wool socks (instead of cotton), a down jacket, a bear canister, and micro-spikes to slip over my sneakers. In the pile to send home is my water filter because it's heavy, bulky, and slow to use. I swore I'd never use a chemical purifier but the chems are quick, easy, and light. I rationalize that it's only for a few months. The other big change is food. I plan to

take lots of it because I want to hike 145 miles before re-supplying, which is further than my usual 85 - 100 mile sections.

There are dozens of backpackers hanging out around the store. I recognize no one. I got out of synch with the flow of hikers I'd been with when I left to go home. My hiker friends are all at least a week (100-plus miles) ahead of me. After two days at Kennedy Meadows, it occurs to me that I'll be going into the Sierras alone. This absolutely was not the plan. I always thought I'd be hiking through the snowy mountains with others, but everyone here is solidly locked into groups formed weeks ago. The notion of hiking alone through the mountains is jarring. How on earth will I do it? I reframe the situation as an opportunity to practice deep self-reliance but still, the prospect of going into the snowy mountains alone is unnerving.

Years ago when I first laid eyes on the Sierras, it was love at first sight. Brought up in the east, I had no idea such a place existed. I came to the Sierras in my early 20's to work for the summer and stayed for six years. The beauty and peace I found in these mountains felt like a miracle. The Sierras set me free, allowing the beginning of an irrepressible joy to emerge. I fell deeply in love with granite peaks, with rock climbing and trail running. I fell in love with waterfalls, dipper birds, giant sequoias, deer, marmots, and with skinny-dipping under full moons. I fell in love with a man, and with an entire community of people who had a similar reaction and passion for these mountains. But that was a long time ago. I have no experience backpacking through snow or fording fast-moving rivers. These are the thoughts swirling through my brain as I walk down the road to spend my last night in a campground before venturing into the deep unknown.

My backpack in extremely heavy. The straps dig into my

shoulders, making it difficult to walk. I'm carrying ten days of food and extra winter gear. There was a scale at the General Store. I arrived with a 22-pound pack, and left with it weighing 42 pounds. Not good. At dinner I eat as much as I can to help lighten my load.

June 14
An older gentleman is walking toward me on the trail. I don't follow PCT buzz but even I've heard about Billy Boy. He's pushing 80, has a long white beard, and has logged about a million miles on the PCT. He floats his way down the trail and upon arrival, talks nonstop. He tells me about the trees, birds, and rocks he's been noticing and about how he never carries a bear canister and how he uses his food bag as a pillow. "Bears like drainages. If you never camp in one you'll be fine." He tells me he used to work for the MBTA in Boston. "Today is a very fine day!" he nods, and then drifts away.

A mile later a pool of sparkling water whispers my name. I strip and jump in. The icy water knocks the wind out of me. I dunk my head under the shimmering surface, allowing it to baptize me. I'm home. I've arrived. I'm in my beloved Sierras.

June 15 – 17
During the next few days, I scramble over rocks, trudge through snow and teach myself how to ford turbulent creeks. I never take chances when it comes to creek crossings. This time of year snow from high peaks melts quickly, causing creeks to swell and creating powerful currents. Sometimes it takes over an hour to find a good spot to cross. My mantra at such times is, "You are alone. Be careful. Don't take any chances."

I give myself over completely to the mountains. I get used to the cold, get used to constantly having wet feet, and get used to never seeing anyone. I breathe thin, clean air and drink clear, delicious water. I watch wildlife and waterfalls, and with each step that I take, I climb higher and deeper into the snowy wilderness. Until I reach a place where everything is frozen, snow crystals glitter, and the cobalt sky is so close, I can almost touch it.

By the fourth night I've walked 71 miles and am camped near Tyndell Creek. I spent most of today playing hide and seek with the trail, which was often hidden beneath five feet of snow. My tent is pitched on a dry patch of granite. It's 9 p.m. but there's still enough light to see Forester Pass in the distance. I'll climb it tomorrow.

I'm camped at 11,500' and it's very cold. I get into my sleeping bag wearing all of my clothes, including gloves, hat, and scarf. I walked 20 miles today—a huge distance in these mountains—and forded several creeks. I'm extremely cold but sleep comes easily anyway. I wake up a lot during the night feeling cold, and each time hug the bag closer to my body. My dreams are intense and vivid. Just before dawn, I dream that I'm in the Himalayas about to tackle Everest. In the dream, I'm terribly cold and trying to sleep before the expedition, when I hear footsteps crunching on frozen snow. A woman's voice says, "Hello. Good Morning! Hello. Who's in there?" I wake up and realize the voice is not a dream! There's a woman standing outside my tent!

I haven't seen anyone in these immense, incredible mountains for over four days! As I unzip the tent, my face comes nose-to-knee with two sets of red ski pants. I follow the red legs up until I find their rightful owners, a man and a woman. My rusty vocal cords squeak out "Hello." They introduce themselves as Zoe and Bill, a married couple in their sixties, from New Zealand. Done with introductions, Zoe asks, "Would you like to climb Forester with us?" I respond, "What time is it?" Bill replies, "6 a.m." Without hesitation I say, "No thanks. It's too early. My plan is to sleep until 8:00." I glance at the thermometer. It's 18 degrees.

"Pity," Zoe says, then all four red legs pivot in unison and strut off. As for me, I roll over and go back to the Himalayas.

Red Legs leaving after early morning wake up call.

3

Forester to Belden

....

The snow is melting into music.

~ JOHN MUIR

....

June 18

8 a.m.

In retrospect, it may have been wise to join them. Forester Pass, at 13,200', is the highest point on the PCT and from what I can see from where I'm camped, is completely covered with snow. I place my frozen running shoes in the sun to thaw. When I'm ready to leave, I jam my feet into the still stiff and misshapen shoes. Tonight I'll wrap them inside my pack, maybe that will keep them from freezing.

Tyndell Creek is much lower this morning than it was last night. I don't want to get my socks wet this early in the day so I take off my shoes, peel off my socks, and step barefoot into the creek. The bone-chilling water sends a shock up my body, and the fierce current throws me off balance at first, but luckily I remain standing and am able to cross without issue.

I walk a few miles on a frozen snowfield. When I reach the base of Forester, I stare up at the icy mass, uncertain as to what to do next. How am I supposed to get over this thing? There are several sets of tracks leading toward the pass. I pick a set cut in a tight S pattern, then kick my running shoes (with micro spikes) into the thick glaze of ice covering the snow and follow the tracks up the nearly vertical slope. The higher I get, the more ill at ease I become. I talk out loud to myself: "Don't look down, don't look down, don't look down." Inching my way up the glistening wall, my self-talk turns into a self-shout. "Don't look down! Don't look down! *Don't look down!*" My foot slips and I shove my umbrella into the snow, thinking *"If I had an ice ax, I'd use it right now!"* It takes effort to get up to the pass, but when I arrive at the top it's spectacular. Standing alone, two and a half miles in the sky, mountains unfold in every direction. My heart feels as spacious and clear as the view. I breathe in the joy of being alone atop this mountain, then eat a protein bar and prepare to descend.

View from Forester Pass

Getting down the steep north side of the pass will be tricky. Here's hoping instinct, logic, and luck are on my side. Last fall when I thru-hiked the John Muir Trail, there was zero snow here and it was so much easier! But the payback for being here now is that I get it all to myself. It feels completely mine. Every part of me feels alertly connected to this frozen miraculous world; every part of me feels fully alive. I'm alone trying to figure out how to cross my first snowy pass, surrounded by sharp cliffs, a cobalt blue sky, dry air, and silence.

It seems to make sense to descend along the edge of the lateral ridge below. I walk cautiously toward it, then follow the contours of snow and ice that cover the spur. There's a steep drop-off on my left. I take step after step after step until suddenly, my left leg post-holes and is gone! I'm up to my hips in snow! I struggle to release my left leg from the snow's tight grip and when I finally pull my leg out of the hole, it's shoeless! My shoe is stuck deep down inside the snow pocket, and because all of this is happening on the edge of a cliff, the situation is rather awkward. My shoe is wedged in beyond my reach. I grab my trusty umbrella, slip it down the hole and poke around until it catches a lace and I'm able to lift it out. Shoe on, I continue hiking and make it down and out of the snow by 3:00.

To celebrate, I fire up my stove and have lunch. Tonight will be my fifth night in the Sierras and already my food supply is low. The cold temperatures and extra effort required to hike at high elevations have increased my appetite and most of my food is gone. Plus, there's the TVP issue (textured vegetable protein). I've eaten it on previous trips and it's been OK, but this time I can't stomach it. It's a great source of lightweight protein, or would be, if I could eat it, but there's no way I can convince myself to touch it. I tried it the other night and couldn't even eat two bites. This is a predicament since my plan is to eat it every other night for dinner. Five out of ten dinners are supposed to be TVP.

I boil up the last of my noodles while a nearby creek provides background music, and a dodgy little squirrel provides company. I eat every last morsel, pack up, and walk to Vidette Meadow, then on to Bubb's Creek where I meet the New Zealanders again. Zoe is sitting cross-legged under a tarp with a desolate look on her face. She's holding a five-pound block of neon orange cheese. I haven't seen a hunk of cheese that big in years. My mouth waters as I stare at it resting in her arms, pleading to be eaten. She cradles it close to her chest as we speak. I can't help but notice that not even a nibble is gone, and marvel at her capacity to carry copious amounts of food in the wilderness. She tells me they're getting off the trail tomorrow to re-supply. Holy cow, all that cheese and they're re-supplying tomorrow? How do they do it? They're amazing! "I don't feel so good" she says, "I can't eat at high elevations." That explains it. I, on the other hand, have the opposite problem and try not to indulge myself too deeply in the fantasy of snatching that slab of mouth-watering, hunger-stopping, highly caloric, artificially-colored, condensed glob of processed fat away from her. "I hope you feel better!" I say, and take off to look for a campsite. I mean it, too. Feeling sick in the mountains is miserable. I honestly hope she feels better. I also honestly wish I had some of that cheese.

I have a cup of miso soup for dinner. Normally, I like miso soup. Tonight it's as satisfying as sipping saltwater. I watch the night sky, then drift off to sleep and dream about food: tantalizing french fries, luscious sweet juicy oranges, thick gooey grilled cheese sandwiches lightly browned to perfection, and a horse trough filled with Caesar salad. I wake up starving. My gut growls. I take the cue and instantly decide to hightail it into town. I'll have to hike an additional 18 miles (9 each way) over Kearsarge Pass and then hitch 20 miles or so into the little town of Independence, but I deem this radical act highly necessary. I want food! So much for hiking 145 miles without re-supplying! I can't wait another 65 miles. The thought of eating pizza and a giant salad by the end of the day is more than I can resist. I happily get on the trail and zoom toward town. The trail to Kearsarge is breathtaking, that is until I lose it and end up climbing the side of a rocky mountain, one boulder at a time. I reach the top of the ridge, hoist myself onto it, and am greeted by two climbers having lunch. They're as startled to see me, as I am to see them. We're south of the pass. I glance down the eastern slope and see a dozen people trudging up a snowy path. Day hikers! I say good-bye to the climbers, and to five and a half days of almost complete solitude, then make my way across the ridge, down the path, and into town.

I must never forget these first few days in the Sierras, a place I dreaded to go alone. I want to remember that among the silence and solitude of these mountains, I climbed, bumped, skidded, splashed, and walked into a place far bigger than myself, far bigger than my thoughts, far bigger than my sense of time and space. Everything I sensed was magnified through a lens of clear alpine air, bounced off granite peaks, and sent straight back to me. If I felt fear, fear came to me in spades. If I felt joy, that's what resonated off of every squirrel, every star, every stone. Nothing stood between what I felt, and what these mountains gave back to me.

June 21
The tiny town of Independence served up food, food, and more food. I spent one night in a motel and the next in a campground

near the trail. Today, I want to walk as far as I can because it's summer solstice, the longest (and my most favorite) day of the year!

Summer Solstice. Two hikers near Glen Pass.

On the way to Glen Pass, I trek through several wide snow bowls situated high above a series of frozen turquoise lakes. I reach the pass and am surrounded by an unceasing array of jagged peaks. I pause briefly before pushing my way through a layer of knee-deep powdery snow, and inch my way down the incredibly steep north side. I see a bright red fuel canister on the white snow and reach for it, simultaneously knocking my water bottle out my pack. I watch as it skips down the side of the mountain. This prompts me to pay closer attention to my footing so that my fate does not mirror that of my water bottle. The drop-off is very steep and with every step

I become more and more uncomfortable. I can't wait to get off this mountain. I force myself to keep my eyes on my feet because when I look up I'm overwhelmed. I don't want to fall. I focus and breathe, focus and breathe, focus and breathe, and get past the steepest section, then relax enough to squat and slide down the rest of the way. I turn to look back and see three people—three tiny specks—slowly negotiating their way down the pass.

Rae Lake

At Rae Lake, I blissfully consume an early dinner: eggs (hard boiled in town), crackers with cream cheese, carrots, half an avocado, and a chocolate chip cookie with tea for dessert. It starts to rain and I take refuge under a scrubby little pine. After an hour I find my way back to the trail and pass two tents belonging to the three specks I saw earlier coming down Glen Pass. I chat with

Audi, a thru-hiker with a thick German accent and dark brown eyes. He tells me that his two friends, Rain and Bluebird, are in their tent and that Bluebird wants to leave the trail. She flew here from Colorado two days ago to join Rain for a week. Today was her first day on the trail and coming down Glen freaked her out. I don't blame her. We've all been on the trail for months and in the Sierras for a week. If I started my hike today with this pass, I'd want out too.

I find the trail and it's submerged under a foot of water, but who cares? I slosh along happily—at least it's a trail and at least I know I'm going in the right direction, something I'm rarely certain of these days. Eight miles later I arrive at Woods Creek and pitch my tent under a tall pine. Two college-aged guys come over for a chat. They're backpacking for a few days, and when I tell them I'm hiking the PCT one of them leaves, returning with gifts of chocolate, fresh basil, and dill!

They leave and I burrow deep inside my pale blue sleeping bag, grateful once again for the warmth of this wonderful bag. I climbed two snow-covered passes today and walked 21 miles. My body feels fully acclimated to high elevation. Before another thought can enter my mind I sleep…

June 22

The scent of pine permeates the crisp morning air, and the sky is a deep heavenly blue. Today is the 49th day since my mother's death, a significant day in the Buddhist tradition, and I want to honor it by walking without the pressure of a mileage goal. I want to be with today in an easy way. Instead of rushing out of camp like I usually do, I sit in front of my tent with a cup of hot chocolate. Something catches my eye. I turn to my left and see a huge mama bear on all fours walking through my campsite, with a little brown cub toddling behind. Mama is cinnamon-colored and bulky-beautiful as she gracefully lumbers by, with little bear in tow. I watch in amazement and awe, drinking in the gift of their strikingly beautiful presence. Neither one of them pays any attention to me, not even a blink, when I whisper, *"Hi Mom!"*

Early afternoon
Woods Creek is a jumble of wild, churning water that acts more like a river than a creek. A waterfall spills down from the high cliff above, forming a thin stream that flows down toward the creek. I'm sprawled out on a sun-drenched slab of warm granite, watching a hawk soar. I roll over onto my belly to sketch and hum and eat not just a rationed wedge of orange, but the entire juicy ball. I gradually make my way back to the trail. In less than a mile the green vegetation gives way to soft snow, roughly four feet deep. I post-hole for quite a long time: step, sink, lift. Step, sink, lift. Step, sink, fall, push myself up. Over and over I do this until I arrive at the base of Pinchot Pass. It's three o'clock and I've only hiked six miles. I stop for the day anyway, and find a dry, flat spot cluttered with sharp black rock chips to camp on. At least there's no snow, everywhere else is covered with deep snow. High above, an uneven ridge forms a semi-circle that stretches east around a wide basin. I climb onto a boulder for tea.

Hours later, when the sun finally sets, all is aglow in an orange-pink light. The big moon glides up over the choppy ridge as I create an altar and put Mom's picture on it. Her gentle hazel eyes watch as I collect tiny pebbles, each one representing a nugget of love—friends, family, teachers—people I want with me, in this remote mountain sanctuary, for her ceremony.

I place the stones in front of the altar and take my seat among them. We sit draped in the glow of soft waning light. When I die, I hope my spirit touches down on a landscape like this before it dissolves into the next way of being. The next place, the next life. There is a next, right? The moon continues to rise. A small grey bird flits in and out of a nearby bush, then perches on a thin branch and begins to sing. I strike a match and take the flame to my mother's chest, watching as it crawls up her throat, melting her cheeks, her eyes, her forehead, her hair. Ashes drift to the ground. I scrape them into a small hole then place a rock on top to mark her grave. I sit with my pebble-friends under the now bluish-black sky. Stars appear. The little bird stops singing. I hear only silence, and a steady pulse emanating from inside the frozen earth.

Moonrise on 49th Day

June 23

On the north side of Pinchot Pass, I sink up to my hips in soft snow. There are only two more high passes to climb before re-supplying at Muir Trail Ranch. After MTR, nothing will be this hard (or so I think). I'll be on Easy Street. After MTR it's just a mere 49 miles to Red's Meadow, and a meager 28 to Lyell Canyon, at which point I should be out of the snow for good!

I post-hole for hours not knowing exactly where I'm going, praying that I'm not too far off-course. I arrive at a river and beg the water gods to let this be the south fork of the Kings River. I walk up the drainage for an hour and luckily, it is. I find the trail. Now all I have to do is figure out how to cross this crazy-wild water.

A thick tree has fallen across the river. I straddle it and push myself along its trunk while water smashes onto my upstream leg. I reach the other side and bask in the sun until I'm warm enough to remove my clothes. I step back in, allowing the water to wash over me, hoping it will take with it the two and a half days of sweat and grime stuck to my body. I submerge my head under the water, then leap out, dry off, and start walking.

Water pours onto the trail from every direction. I slosh along, slowly gaining elevation until everything is frozen again and there are miles of large snow depressions, called sun cups, before me. Walking on sun cups poses an even more challenging task than walking on soft snow, and my progress is impossibly slow. I've seen no one since yesterday morning and am happy to see a hiker ahead of me. When I catch up to him I realize we met 400 miles ago over a game of backgammon. His name is Moe and he tells me that he's done hiking for the day. He'll start out early tomorrow when the sun cups will be firmer and easier to negotiate. I keep walking, slipping, sinking, and falling until I decide his idea is a good one.

I find a patch of dirt for the night, with a view of Mather Pass two miles away. It's 4 p.m., another short day.

Sierra Sun Cups

I'm camped at 11,000 feet and watch with gratitude as my tiny 4-ounce stove lights up fast and hot, even at this elevation. I didn't use the stove much in the desert but in the Sierras I use it every morning for hot coffee and every night for a warm meal. After dinner I organize my gear, do yoga, and then settle in for the night. I pull the drawstring of sleeping bag tightly around my face, and call it a day—another stunning one—in the Sierras.

June 24

I start walking at 6, and Moe was right, it's much easier to walk on sun cups at this time of day. I arrive at the base of Mather and there appears to be only two options: either climb up a long narrow snow chute or crawl up a tumble of rocks to the left of the chute. The snow chute is steep. What if the sun melts it enough to cause an avalanche? My plan is to climb up the rocks and then traverse the top of the chute to the pass. At first things go well, but then it gets a little hairy. My bear canister, which is tied to the top of my pack because it doesn't fit inside, sways each time I lean toward a handhold, and this throws me off balance. I never noticed this issue before, but up here on the rocks where every movement is exaggerated, I constantly have to compensate for the sway.

Three quarters of the way up I get stuck. There's no way to continue without exposing myself to great risk. I hang there clinging to a rock. I'm truly stuck. I look between my feet hoping I can find a way to down-climb. If I can get to the bottom and start over, I'll climb up the snow chute instead. I see no way to down-climb from here. I need to focus my attention on what's in front of me. Meanwhile, my right leg starts vibrating uncontrollably, like its no longer a part of my body—like it has a life of its own. I watch as it bobs furiously up and down. Climbers call this phenomena sewing needle leg. I take my eyes off my shaky leg and stare ahead, trying to figure out what to do. Luckily, all those years (decades ago) spent rock climbing in Yosemite come flooding back to me in muscle memory. My body makes a move and then another, and another, until I'm at the top of the rocky tumble. I traverse the snow chute, safely reach the pass, and pull out a stale bagel to gnaw on, simultaneously vowing never to take such a risk again. I let go of the stress, relax, and admire the view. Four hikers come up the chute and I welcome them cheerfully. This is the first pass I've shared with anyone.

We leave together, glissading our way down the mountain in no time and then split up. I walk by the ecstatically beautiful Palisades Lakes, nestled into a glacial basin, then walk downhill for miles until the trail flattens near Deer Meadow and then climbs up toward Muir Pass. I want to get as close as possible to Muir before stopping for the day. After a long break, I walk until hitting deep snow at 9:00, and camp on a huge rock four miles below the pass. I'm tired, cold and hungry and hastily put up my tent. When I'm fed and settled, I admire the big moon rising over a nearby ridge. I woke today at 11,000', climbed to 12,100', then hiked down to 8,020' and am back up at 11,000'. Tomorrow when I cross Muir I'll gain another 995 feet.

June 25

I'm having breakfast in front of my tent when six New Zealanders arrive on the scene. Zoe looks much better than the last time I saw her, when she was ill and holding a slab of cheese. She introduces the others, pointing out that the leader of their team is an ace navigator. With that in mind, I keenly observe their route as they fade into the snowy horizon. An hour later, I follow their tracks but quickly lose them and get caught in a loop that leads nowhere. Not that it's a total waste of time. It's a stunningly gorgeous loop beside frozen lakes and tall granite spires. I wonder if anyone has ever been back here? Certainly "yes," but to me it feels like the most remote and curious place on earth.

Once back on track, I hike up several false summits, each time thinking, "For sure this is the pass." Though it never is. When I finally arrive at Muir Pass, a plump little marmot greets me. I stop long enough to take a few pictures, then hike down passing Wanda Lake, named after John Muir's older daughter. I passed Helen Lake a few miles back, named for his younger daughter. Did either of them make it here? Surely, they must have.

Wanda Lake

Evolution Basin lies beneath tall, intricately carved granite walls. I walk below the west ridge in deep snow and come to an extremely wide creek. I put my camera, iPod, and cell phone in plastic bags and tuck them deep inside my pack, which is lined with a thick black trash bag. I step into the thigh-deep water. It's painfully cold and the current pushes me precariously back and forth. After the initial shock I focus all my attention on simply staying upright. I don't want to fall. The slime-covered rocks at my feet aren't helping matters, but I make it across, put on dry socks, and keep moving. By the time I get to a section of trail called The Golden Staircase, the snow is gone and a waterfall spews loudly and elegantly beside the path.

Evolution Basin

Forester (13,200'), Glen (11,978'), Kearsarge (11,670'), Pinchot (12,130'), Mather (12,100'), and now Muir (11,955') are done. I know there's still work ahead before reaching Tuolumne: Seldon (10,880'), Silver (10,880'), Donahue (11,060') and plenty of other ups and downs, but I'm making progress and am elated that six big passes are behind me. Tomorrow is my birthday and in a fit of desire, I decide to night hike to Muir Trail Ranch. I walked 18 miles yesterday. If I make it to MTR tonight it will be a 24-mile day. There's a package waiting for me and I'm planning to have an easy day tomorrow. Why not push it tonight?

I practically dance my way across the exquisite soft beauty of McClure Meadow, stopping twice to talk with other hikers before reaching Evolution Creek at 8 p.m. I've been here twice before. Both times it was late September when the creek was nothing more than a simple wade through shin-deep water. Tonight the creek is extremely high, fast, and strong. I hear loud water crashing further down the creek, signifying either a drop-off or very choppy water. I remember the vow I made on top of Mather yesterday (no unnecessary risks) and ditch my night hiking plans. I find a dry, level place to sleep. My boulder bed last night was on a tilt, and even in my amazing sleeping bag, at 11,200' I was incredibly cold. Here, at 9,200' it feels almost balmy and the flat piece of dirt where I plan to put my tent looks like paradise. My night-hiking-in-the-Sierras ambitions will have to wait.

There's a full moon lunar eclipse tomorrow morning at 4:30, a cosmic birthday gift? I set my alarm. This is my 46th night on the trail. Mile 848. I hiked 19 miles today and am as tired as I've ever been in my life, and although I need no help, the sound of dancing water lulls me to sleep. I wake for the lunar eclipse, but high cliffs block my view.

June 26
Standing on the bank of Evolution Creek, the water doesn't look any easier to cross this morning than it did last night. After much scrutiny, I step in and instantly get knocked facedown into

the current. I easily grab a branch and pull myself out. It's not a problem except for now I'm sopping wet and cold. The New Zealanders appear and mention that there's an easy crossing a mile back. We all turn around, find it, and cross. It's a piece of cake. Cold, waist-high water—yes, but with only a mild current.

Colorful wildflowers escort me for next five miles. Color! I haven't seen wildflowers since the desert! I cross Piute Creek on a wooden bridge and before I know it, I'm at Muir Trail Ranch. Mattie, the owner, is a salty old bird in her 80's with deep lines on her face and a devilish twinkle in her eye. She points to the bright orange five-gallon paint bucket with my name on it. The bucket is an MTR requirement, as is the $75 fee to have them pick it up at the post office. I pry off the lid and tear into food nirvana, then spend a relaxing day by the San Joaquin River.

June 27

After a day of rest, I'm up early and raring to go. I climb out of the river drainage and four miles later, drop my pack and do 25 pushups and 100 sit-ups. My lower body is rock solid but I'm losing weight and tone in my upper body. Maybe this will help. At Sally Keyes Lakes I meet three weekenders sitting on folding chairs set in front of spacious tents. I have breakfast at the lake and then "sally" forth to Seldon Pass, which even with a deep layer of snow, is an easy one. I take pictures of Marie Lake and of the snow-covered peaks beyond. I don't take another picture for 300 miles.

I walk along the western shore of frozen Marie Lake until the snowy trail turns to mud. The sun is warm and the sky is that intensely beautiful cobalt blue again. I feel completely at home in these mountains; every ounce of my thinning body is filled with joyous anticipation. I walk a few miles and reach a fast-moving creek that gives me pause, but not worry. How many creeks have I forded in the past ten days? 30? 50? Some have been wide, some narrow, all of them cold. This is just another creek. Upstream the water narrows and smashes over giant rocks, I can't cross there. Downstream the water widens and deepens.

I grab two branches to use as walking sticks and go back to where the trail dips into the creek. I face upstream, take a deep breath, relax, and side step into the water. I take a second step, and am knocked off my feet and swept facedown into the current. I'm stunned. Did this really happen? The current is powerful. My legs bang up against rocks as I'm pushed swiftly along. My pack is clipped tightly at both my hip and chest. They say it's best to have your pack unclipped when fording, because if you get sucked in it's easier to release an unclipped pack and swim to shore. Because my bear canister throws me off balance, I always keep my pack clipped.

At first I'm calm. I'm moving fast and getting whacked by rocks, but I'm calm. I have no control and get sucked into deep water. As this is happening, items from my pack float rapidly by: my hat, a tube of sun block, my bandana. I remain calm and think, "This is okay. Things are okay. I'll just get out." I try as hard as I can to swim to shore but can't. The current is too strong and rocks keep smacking me. After several futile attempts I think, "Oh crap. This is serious." My mind spins as I remember a time, long ago, when my friend Josh and I were hiking above Yosemite Falls and he got swept in. I was standing on a bridge watching as he leaned into the creek to get water and was pulled in and pushed down to the edge of the falls. Just before going over he clung to a rock, and that saved his life.

Remembering this, I furiously grab at rocks and manage to wrap my arms around one but it's slimy and the current is so forceful I can't hold on, not even for a moment. The current pushes me down the creek very fast and I get more and more banged up. I think of my friend again and about how he said that if you ever get caught in a strong current, don't fight it, swim to the side. I try this but it doesn't work, at least not right away. I keep trying to get to the side of the creek, until suddenly a fierce physical determination takes over my body. It's a kind of will I've never known before. With all my body, and all my heart, and all the energy that has ever passed through me in this lifetime, I will myself out of the water. I don't know whether I say the words out loud, or if it's just one giant shout inside my head, but I keep repeating with deep body force: *"I want to live! I want to live! I want to live!"* I see a thin yellow willow branch reaching out to me like a long bony finger, and grasp it. I cling on to it for dear life as water rages around me. God Bless the meager-looking willow branch! That thin, spindly finger is much stronger than it appears. I hang on, and when I trust that it can handle my weight, I haul myself out the water. I'm pretty beat up but alive, and although most of my body is battered, luckily I didn't hit my head.

My body heaves and sobs uncontrollably as I empty my pack on the small island I've landed on. Everything is soaked. I didn't wrap anything because the creek didn't look like that much of a threat. My camera is dead. I pull out the memory card out, hoping it will survive. My phone is dead and my watch has stopped. I sob but keep moving. I lay out clothes and gear to dry on rocks, bushes, and tree branches. I start shaking and inspect the cuts and bruises on my legs, back, hip and chest. There's a gash on my left shin with a lump that's growing before my eyes into a swollen little mountain. I'm very upset. I should eat something, nourish my body. I eat a few trail bars and drink a half-liter of water. I take ibuprofen, put antibacterial cream on the gash, and find a patch of snow near a tree. I pile snow onto my swollen leg and tie it in place with a shirt. My back hurts. I lie on the snow thinking the cold will help ease the pain and reduce the swelling that I feel building near my lower spine. I elevate both legs by leaning them against the tree trunk. It's 2:00. I stay like this for the next three hours, packing and re-packing snow on my body, keeping my legs elevated, eating, and drinking.

I didn't come to these mountains for this. I didn't come here to risk my life or to hurt my body. I haven't seen anyone since the happy weekenders I met before breakfast. It's time to figure out what to do next. The best way to get off the island and the shortest distance to shore will bring me back to where I started. You've got to be kidding? All this and I don't even get to be on the other side? Cautiously, I step into the water and make my way to shore. It hurts to walk but at least it's possible. I walk slowly downstream to see if I can find a safe place to cross. I walk for an hour and find nothing. I walk upstream as far as I can but am stopped by the same thundering water that stopped me before.

Usually, I stealth camp but tonight I put my tent right out in the open, beside the trail. I want to be seen in case someone comes by. I tell myself that I won't mention what happened to just anyone. Personalities on the trail are a microcosm of personalities in the real world. There are people you instantly bond with and people you instinctively steer clear of. If some good people show up and we cross the creek together, then I'll continue on the PCT. I don't have high hopes for this happening. I can go for days in the Sierras without seeing a soul. I create an exit plan. I'll turn around in the morning and hike back to Muir Trail Ranch and from there I'll hike out of the mountains and go home. I've had enough. I have nothing to prove. 869 miles is a good enough hike.

I eat dinner and tend to my wounds. All night I listen to the noisy creek. It sounds hostile and unkind. I'm angry at it. I don't want to be angry. I don't want the lovely sound of energetic water, a sound I've always adored, to now be something I bristle against, rage at, and avoid, but that water hurt me. It nearly stole my life. All night long I lie inside my tent aching and sore, trying in vain to make peace with Bear Creek.

June 28

5:30 a.m.

"Good morning!" sing two heavily-accented female voices. I scramble from my tent as fast as I can and meet two women with long dark wavy hair, bright clear eyes, and huge smiles. Siddi and Sarah are from Israel. A few moments later their friend from the U.S., Alec, joins us. He, too, is happy, bright-eyed, and kind. They're all in their early twenties. "Would you like to cross the creek with us? Can we help you take down your tent?" I've said nothing to them except "Hello." I can't believe my good fortune. "Yeah, sure," I respond, "That would be great! Let's take the tent down; let's cross together."

Within minutes it's clear I can trust them but I say nothing as we walk toward the creek. We inspect the water. I feel uncomfortable with the idea of getting back in. Someone comments on the strong current and I spill the beans. I tell them that this is where I tried to cross yesterday, and show them my bruised legs and spine. We move downstream.

A tall, heavyset man on the other side of the creek steps in. He wobbles from knee-high water to waist-high water in only a few steps but maintains his balance. He climbs out of the hole and teeters his way over to us. Alec drops his gear, and does a test crossing, confirming the route we'll take. Siddi and Sarah go first. They step in and face up-stream. Siddi holds Sarah's waist and

Sarah grips onto her hiking poles. Six points of contact. They side-step across, all the while laughing and joking, making the whole thing look easy and fun! Now it's our turn. Alec and I step into the water. He shouts over his shoulder "Hey, if at any point you feel uncomfortable and want to get out, let me know. We'll go back. Okay?" Could I be with better people? Without a doubt: No. We make our way across. I'm certain my hike would have ended today if it weren't for them. We say good-bye and I fire up my stove. A backpacker camped on the ledge above comes down and we drink tea together. He tells me he's a local and is up here camping for a few days. Then he says, "Every year someone dies in this creek."

Two miles beyond Bear Creek, Orca is sitting on a rock with a desolate look on his face. He's a strong guy in his late twenties with long, curly, reddish-blonde, hippie hair, a scruffy beard, and a charming smile. He's easy to talk to, and a good listener. I think every woman on the trail has a crush on him. Every time I see him he's with a different woman, but today he's alone. He says he's having a rough time because he's out of food and exhausted. After the kindness just extended to me, I eagerly pass him my food bag, "Take anything you want."

My body hurts. It's difficult to move but I figure I'll get used to it. I'll heal faster if I keep moving. With every step I take, my pack thumps the tender area on my lower spine causing a sharp pain to shoot through my body. I pad my back with a rolled up shirt. This helps somewhat. I take it easy. I don't move fast but I move and I keep moving. Later in the day, I meet the Israelis hanging out by the bridge near Edison Lake. Alec went across the lake to re-supply and has just returned. We hike up the north fork of Mono Creek and camp under a stormy sky. I listen to the girls laugh and laugh and laugh as I doze.

June 29

6:30 a.m.

The north fork of Mono Creek has a reputation for being difficult
to cross this time of year. The water has tremendous force, but it's
narrow and we cross without issue. I forded five creeks yesterday
and now Mono is out of the way. My creek-crossing confidence is
returning. We walk up and over Silver Pass with its endless views
of snow-capped peaks, then slide our way down to Squaw Lake. I
say good-bye to my friends and set my sights on Red's Meadow,
21 miles away. I walk most of the day under tall trees that shield
the sun, keeping the snow firm and cold and easy to walk on. The
trail drops into a lush green meadow kept moist by a long curling
stream, to a place called Tully Hole. I stop here for an early dinner
and make a point of drinking two full liters of water mixed with
electrolytes. I'm going to night hike to Red's. I have a cup of coffee
to prepare myself for the climb up to Virginia and Purple Lakes. I
know I'll hit snow again and it will be slow-going, but I want out.
I want out of these mountains as soon as possible. I pack up and
climb a long series of switchbacks that lead to the alpine lakes.

At twilight the air is cool. I dig into the side pocket of my pack
for a hat to pull over my ears. I walk as the sun sinks below the
horizon, casting a purple hue upon the snow. I walk until the sky
is black and the mountains disappear into the night. I walk until a
hundred thousand stars appear. I walk sensing wild things behind
rocks and trees. I can hear them breathe. I walk and walk and walk
without ever stopping. I walk on snow at times, but thankfully, I
walk mostly on dry trail. The night is very black. My pack thumps
my sore lower back. I adjust the shirt as best I can and keep walking.

At 10:00 it's back to deep snow. I cross and re-cross the same
narrow creek many times. A part of me marvels that I can creek-

cross at night just two days after my dunk. Another part of me wonders if I should stop. I keep moving. I've been moving for seven hours, focused on only one thing: getting out of here. I'm hungry to get out. I need to get out. I want to rest and re-group. I want a bath and a bed. I want to heal my body.

The moon rises and guides me the last few miles. When I arrive at Red's Meadow, I peer through the store window at a round-faced clock. It's midnight. I hiked 27 tough miles today with a sore body and a mind that couldn't stop thinking about getting tossed around in Bear Creek. I can't believe I made it out of that water alive. I can't believe I made it here. I toss my bag on the ground. Unable to sleep I wait for dawn and at first light, I go to the café. When it opens, I shovel pancakes into my weary body, and then take a bus into Mammoth.

June 30 – July 2

As the bus passes Mammoth Mountain, skiers glide down the trails. I find a comfortable hotel in town and spend most of my time soaking in Epsom salt, sleeping, and talking with a close friend back east. I attempt to replace my camera but there are no good options in this small town. I go to Mammoth Mountaineering Supply (one of the best mountaineering shops on the trail) and replace the other items I've lost. While I'm there, I have a casual conversation with an employee. Without getting into details, I hint at what happened and he gets it. He strongly encourages me to continue, saying that over the years he's seen all kinds of hikers pass through and heard all kinds of stories. He tells me I had my "moment" and that it's over. Things will only get better, he assures me.

Never underestimate the power of a sincere response, even from a stranger. After three days of good sleep, healthy food, and enough time to begin the healing process, I conclude that, "*Of course*, I'll get back on the trail! *Of course*, I'm walking to Canada!" I get myself back to Red's Meadow and cough up 20 bucks to stay at a crowded, noisy campground. It feels strange to pay for camping after so many nights sleeping under the stars for free. I get comfortable in my campsite and watch with amazement as a van pulls up to the site next to mine and a young couple with a small child unloads their gear. I try not to stare as they haul out tables, chairs, a swing, a TV, a mansion-sized tent, a boom box, and six coffin-sized ice chests. I ask how long they're staying and the husband replies, "Two nights." They ask me why I'm alone and carrying so little. Clearly, they're not impressed with my answer. They are friendly and we plan to have hot chocolate together after dinner, though somehow this never happens. I have a restless night listening to cars come and go, and can't wait to get back to the trail.

July 3

After breakfast I walk 13 miles and camp on a ridge with a gorgeous view of Thousand Island Lake. Normally I would have whizzed right by this lovely spot, hiking as late as possible into the night. But today I walk easy, stopping early, taking care to allow my body to mend.

July 4

There's snow on Island Pass and more snow on Donahue, which is the final pass before Tuolumne Meadows. On the west side of Donahue, I ford a gentle creek and camp near six southbound John Muir Trail (JMT) hikers. Between the six of them (five guys, one girl) they have an enormous amount of food. One of them gifts me with an entire package of Rivita crackers laced with nuts, seeds, and raisins. From that moment on, they become my favorite trail staple.

We sit around a blazing fire (my only campfire on the entire trail!) surrounded by miraculous mountains, telling stories late into the night.

July 5

In the morning, I walk through a lush green canyon—my prize for having made it through the High Sierras, mostly alone, and mostly in one piece. Lyell Canyon is eight miles long and a river runs gently through it. There are swimming holes galore! I stop a few times to splash around, and arrive at the backpacker's campground by noon.

The man behind the counter at the miniscule Tuolumne Meadows Post Office proudly announces that this is the only post office in America open today, Monday, July 5th, a federal holiday. I'm grateful for this because I ordered a replacement tent (zipper gave out) and it's here. The mosquitoes can be nasty in Yosemite, so I'm thrilled it has arrived. I also receive hiking poles sent from home. I can't believe I chose not to use them until now. I had them in the beginning, but sent them home because I didn't like using them. Poles are particularly helpful when fording because the tips can wedge between river rocks better than a walking stick, thereby improving stability. They may not have saved me from Bear Creek—many people using poles get knocked into creeks—but I look forward to using them now.

The gash on my leg doesn't look good. I haven't been able to keep it dry and because of that, it's not healing. It needs to stay dry. I spend two nights in Tuolumne resting, cleansing the wound, and watching for signs of infection.

One evening I go to the amphitheater for a ranger talk and he tells a story about a bear that recently broke into his car. He claims the bear broke in because it smelled a salt packet inside the trunk. That's why the bear tore his car apart? I can't believe my ears. Can this possibly be true? A salt packet? Really? I can't help thinking that the ranger must have forgotten to mention that the salt packet was stuck onto a rotisserie chicken.

The next day I get a ride to the town of Lee Vining, located 13 miles east of the park. The town has a wonderful visitor center with a great bookshop, a funky coffee shop, and a well stocked little market. Lee Vining is also home to Mono Lake, a saline lake that provides a critical nesting area for migratory birds. Odd-looking rock formations called tufa, made of limestone, protrude several feet out of the water. I spend the afternoon wandering near the shore, and watching birds, mesmerized by the magic of this exotic high desert world.

July 7

I'm excited about the next 78-mile section, from Tuolumne to Sonora Pass. At 4 p.m. I get on the trail and walk for a few hours. I pitch my tent on a hill, with views of glacier-carved granite mountains. I think about the ranger, the bear story, and the car that got ripped apart because of a salt packet? I sleep well, anyway, and spend the next day exploring the enchanting Matterhorn Canyon. I see no one in this deliriously beautiful place. At dusk I follow the trail down to a swampy bog, where it disappears into the muck. My feet get soaked as I step onto a soggy island. It's getting dark and I don't want to spend the night in this creepy place. I backtrack (which I hate to do), find a lovely spot and put up the tent as mosquitoes hungrily attack. My body is healing. It's still sore and bruised, but it's healing. I hiked 22 miles today.

July 8

I'm camped high above Stubblefield Canyon. A stunning array of mountains and canyons unfold below. A few steps away from my camp, a thin stream flows over warm granite, creating a private hot tub (it's warmish), big enough for me to soak in. It's unbelievably gorgeous, the weather is warm, and the water is plentiful. Surely, this must be heaven.

Trail Notes:

- Bear Creek stole my mojo. Matterhorn Canyon gave it back.
- As I write, there are at least 5,000 mosquitoes clinging to the mesh walls of my tent. 30,000 bug legs.
- I didn't bring fuel for this section. If I don't miss my stove I'll bounce (hiker term for mail) it to Oregon.
- Much to my surprise, I'm getting used to trekking poles. I actually like them now.

Dinner:

Appetizer: Carrots dipped in freshly ground almond butter.

Main Course: Hummus, black olives, capers, string beans, chili peppers, and fresh basil on Rivita crackers.

Dessert: Organic dates.

July 11

It takes me two rides to hitch 28 miles from Sonora Pass to Bridgeport. The first ride is with a chatty, happy, middle-aged couple. They ask a lot of questions and tell me about the family reunion they've just attended. It is a happy, easy ride. The second ride is not.

The happy couple drops me off at Hwy 395, and ten minutes later a tan pickup truck stops. I open the passenger door and a tsunami of intense energy rolls out of the cab and nearly knocks me over. I've never felt anything like this before. The man behind the wheel is clean-cut and looks to be around forty. He seems okay. I get in. He tells me he's a marine stationed at the Mountain Warfare Training Center up the road. The air is thick with tension. What's going on? I try to engage him in light-hearted conversation but he'll have none of it. He frowns, holds the steering wheel with a white-knuckle grip and gives curt one-word responses to my questions, if he responds at all. He has a sour look on his face. He seems deeply preoccupied and tightly wound up. What happened to him? I don't feel threatened but something is clearly not right.

I keep quiet. We drive down the blank highway listening to static on the radio. He's here, but not here. The air is filled with turmoil. I can't wait for this ride to be over, and focus my attention on the mile markers, watching as they slowly pass by. The landscape is dull, cracked and dry. The windshield collects dust and dead bugs. When I see the sign for Bridgeport, I blurt out, "Hey, this is great. I'll get out here." I grab my stuff and walk the rest of the way into town.

I meet some hiker friends and we share a hotel suite. It has two bedrooms, a large living room, a kitchen, and a huge bathroom. It's very nice but I prefer to sleep outside on the deck. Someone has a friend with a car, so getting back to the trail tomorrow will be a snap.

July 12 – 15

At Sonora Pass the trail climbs from 9,600' to 10,500' in less than four miles. The views are phenomenal! The sun is warm, the air cool, and I feel good. It's taken two full weeks to recover, but I finally feel like myself again as I happily walk toward South Lake Tahoe.

A few hours later I meet some southbound hikers who "flipped," meaning they jumped ahead and are walking back. The flippers left the Sierras at Kennedy Meadows, hopped a bus to the Oregon border, and are hiking south. When they reach the High Sierras, most of the snow will be gone and the creeks will be easier to negotiate. Not a bad plan. I can't help thinking that maybe I should have done that too.

Over the next three days I hike 20, 20, and 23 miles. On the fourth day I hike only 13 miles, then rent a tent-cabin at Berkeley Camp, where I share showers, laundry, and the dining hall with 150 teenagers from the city. I can see a tiny patch of beautiful Lake Tahoe from my tent-cabin.

At the general store I buy two ears of organic corn and eat them on the spot. My new camera has arrived, along with some packages from home. Orca is sitting in front of the store with three female admirers. He shows me the video he took yesterday of a bear playing with his food canister. Bears? I just mailed my canister home. I carried it from Mile 702 to Mile 1089 (387 miles) and am happy to be rid of the additional bulk and weight. Watching his video makes me wonder if I should've kept it longer.

July 16, 17

The trail is crowded with day hikers. It's nice to have company after so much time alone, but wow, so many people. Aloha Lake is an easy walk and a small price to pay for such exquisite beauty. No wonder it's crowded. I meet a bunch of boy scouts and their leaders and have lunch with them. Later, I see some hiker friends and camp two nights with them. As we approach Squaw Valley I'm excited to be walking on part of the Western States 100, an ultra trail running event held every June.

I take a wrong a turn down a steep sandy path and skid my way down to a road. My shoes have no tread left on them. I've worn them for the past 500 miles, plus they already had a hard 250 miles on them when I picked them up at Kennedy Meadows. They served me very well, but are now in shreds. My legs and feet feel fine but it's definitely time for new shoes!

I spend the night at Donner Pass with Trail Angels. They're kind and helpful to the nine of us staying with them. After my shower I step on the scale and am alarmed to see that I've lost 18 pounds, which is 15% of my body weight. My weight never varies by more than a pound or two. If I keep this up, I'll disappear by the time I get to Canada. This is not good. I tend to eat sparingly on the trail and make up for it by gorging in town. At home after a hard workout I eat endlessly. On the trail after a hard workout I eat a cup of beans. Apparently, this strategy is not working. The number glaring up at me is a number I haven't seen between my toes since junior high school. I must change my poor eating habits. At dinner I skip salad and eat pasta, chicken, potatoes, pie, and ice cream. I stuff myself.

I order shoes online, and then get a ride into town. At the grocery store I buy calorie-rich food: olive oil, avocados, cheese, and peanut butter. When I return to the house, I douse a bowl of cold pasta with oil, eat every bite, and then sprawl out under the stars.

Shoe History
Pair 1 - Campo, CA to Tehachapi, CA, 550 miles
Pair 2 - Tehachapi, CA to Kennedy Meadows, CA, 150 miles
(didn't like them, left them in hiker box)

Pair 3 - KM to Sierra City, CA, 500 miles plus 250 (from previous hike)
Pair 4 - Sierra City, CA to Trout Lake, WA, 1,040 miles
Pair 5 - Trout Lake, WA to Manning Park, CAN, 418 miles

July 18
It's only 42 miles to Sierra City. Two days, one night. I pick a campsite high on a ridge covered with hundreds of marsh marigolds. Their long leaves and yellow daisy-like faces feel strangely alive. Humanly alive, like in the Wizard of Oz. I half-expect them to break out in song.

July 19 – 21
I meet a woman on the trail who asks what I'm doing. When I tell her I've been on the trail since the Mexican border and am heading to Canada, she shrieks, *"Aren't you afraid? Are you carrying a gun?"* I'm not quite sure how to respond. Yes to afraid, and no to gun? Or, sometimes yes, and definitely not? Or, had more fear in the beginning, and less now that the marigolds sing to me at night?

In Sierra City (tiny, tiny, tiny, Sierra City) I camp in the backyard of the Red Moose Inn. Good people, good food, Internet, and laundry. At the country store I pick up my new shoes (no post office here) and bid a nostalgic farewell to my beat-up sneakers. I slip my feet into my pretty new purple and white shoes and head back to the inn. It feels like I'm walking on air.

July 22 – 25
After hiking 23 miles I camp on the edge of a field and the next morning wake to a hole in front of my tent. It's roughly two feet long, a foot wide and four inches deep. Who was scratching at my

door? I didn't hear a thing.

I walk all day and into the night and camp on a sandy beach beside the Feather River. The next day I push my way through miles of trail covered with overgrown vegetation. At dusk I see a sign for Trail Angels and spend the night with them at Buck's Lake. I eat well and have fun—though this is the last time I stay with Angels because I want to stay on the trail as much as possible from here to the finish.

I've walked 1,270 miles and still have 430 miles to go before reaching the Oregon border. California is way too big! I mean it. This state is too big. I can't wrap my mind around the fact that I'm still walking in the same state I started in three months ago. I meet a southbound section hiker who asks me how things are going. He seems like a nice guy so I tell him the truth. I tell him things are feeling a little tedious. No, things aren't feeling a little tedious, things are feeling extremely tedious, flat, dull, boring, endless and on top of that, the scenery isn't all that great. He says he met a thru-hiker yesterday who looked as worn out as me, and she said the very same thing. He suggests I do a little yoga and meditate. I maintain a blank expression on my face, but inwardly roll my eyes. Yoga and meditate? Yeah, right, who has time for that? I need to keep moving—one step after the other—go, go, go—no stopping, or I'll never get out of this state, never get to Canada. Go, go, go. It's all about moving. Gotta keep moving.

Later I learn there's a term for what I'm experiencing, it's called "The NoCal Blues." Apparently it's not uncommon for thru-hikers to feel flat and discouraged at this stage of the game. For me, it feels like treading water—like I'm going nowhere, like I'll never get out of this (both emotional and physical) state. Plus, the scenery is okay, but nothing like the extraordinary scenery of the previous

500 miles. I nod good-bye to my guru and start hiking, desperately in need of a mood-buster. I notice a creek and allow myself to let go of my thru-hiker instinct of always wanting to be on the move. I immerse my body in its shallow waters, then dry off, do a little yoga, and meditate.

When that's done, I meander down the trail toward Belden, escorted by puffy white clouds overhead, and an abundance of poison oak by my side. There's not much in Belden, not even a gas station (that I can see). There's one small restaurant, but I've run out of cash so can't take advantage of it, and walk longingly by as I head up the road. I make camp on the side of a hill, hidden among the trees, on a perch behind the post office. Dogs howl forlornly in the distance. Cars speed by on the skinny highway below. The black night descends, enveloping me with a sense of unease. I'm hungry. I feel hollow and empty inside. A train chugs lethargically by, as I wait for sleep.

4

Belden to Oregon

Everything changes; everything is connected;
pay attention. Pay attention.
~ JANE HIRSHFIELD

July 26, 27

The population of Belden is 22, down from a population of 26 ten years ago. The post office is located in a small brown house. I step into the living room and am directed to the dining room, where three boxes await me. I'm expecting one, the other two boxes are surprises from home. I had six Oreo cookies for dinner last night (*ran out of food!*), so eagerly haul the booty outside, drop it on the lawn, and tear into it like a feral beast. I eat without thinking—consuming whatever I see. I eat tortilla chips, chocolate bars, applesauce, popcorn, tofu strips, cupcakes, crackers, and cheese. I eat from this box, that one, then the other. I gorge until the hungry beast inside me is sated, bored, and stumbles off to rest. When I return to my senses, I gather my gear, and begin the long, tough climb out of Belden.

My exit is not a graceful one. The heat is wicked, my stomach is confused, and the pack is painfully heavy. The beast in me ate way too much, way too fast. I come close to tossing my cookies (the ones in my stomach, not in my pack) several times, as I slog up the dry, rocky trail. I manage to knock off five miles, but refuse to take another step when I see an appealing spot in the shade. I spread my ground cloth on the earth, and lie flat on my back waiting for nausea to pass.

Belden Post Office

Three guys appear on the trail, and I shout, *"Do you need any food?"* They beeline over and introduce themselves as Nightmare, Nick, and Jalapeño; they're all in their late-twenties. Nightmare is particularly happy with the high quantity of food I'm dispensing.

He says he's trying to hike between 40 and 50 miles a day. In exchange for food he offers me No Doze.

An attractive woman zooms by, and Nightmare eyes her. He says she's attempting to break the PCT speed record. He gets up abruptly and chases after her. When Nick and Jalapeño leave, I spend the rest of the day not moving and not eating. By 5:30, I feel better. I have a cup of coffee, toss the No Doze into the fire ring, and start walking.

The terrain is steep and there are a lot of blow-downs. Someone used the term "blow-down" on Day One of this hike, at the Mexican border. I had no idea what he was talking about. But as I hoist myself over giant trees that have blown down onto the trail, I get it. Once in a while it's possible to walk around an uprooted tree, though the forest is jungle-like, and I climb over most of them. This makes for very slow-going.

When I reach the ridge it's twilight. There are dirt roads and trails leading in every direction, but no trail blazes. Where to go? I stop to look at the map and slip a bug net over my head, which keeps the mosquitoes off my face but not off my arms and legs. I can't stay here or I'll get eaten alive. I take my best guess and scram, following a dirt path that I hope is the trail. It eventually leads to a burn area. A giant yellow moon hangs above the singed forest like a glow-in-the-dark balloon. It's eerie to be in this scorched land, alone at night. A chill of apprehension crawls up my spine. Then something inside me shifts, and the spooky trees bathed in soft moonlight no longer scare me, but strike me as unspeakably beautiful.

I walk deep into the night, never seeing a blaze or another person. This concerns me. Did I misjudge? Am I on the wrong trail? I reach a dirt road marked with a sign nailed to a tree. It reads: 26N12. My guidebook tells me I should be at Road 26N02, not 12. I must be lost. My mood sinks as I accept my fate. Two golden orbs stare at me from the edge of the woods. Mountain lion? I pop open my umbrella, hoping it will keep this and all other night creatures away. I adjust my headlamp, study the map, and conclude that I'm completely lost. There's a trail across the road that I'm tempted follow, but why get more lost than I already am? I pitch my tent behind a thick row of bushes. It's an extremely quiet night. I can't sleep, unnerved by the thought that I've drifted a long way from the PCT.

I toss and turn until dawn. I hear footsteps, and peer out of my tent just in time to catch a glimpse of two hikers racing by at top speed. I recognize them as a couple I met the other day. Eagle Eye is the oldest thru-hiker on the trail (72); both he and his wife Tinkerbelle have done the trail before. Surely they're not lost! Oh happy day—then neither am I! In a split-second my gloomy mood turns happy. I'm not lost! Go figure. (Turns out it was a typo in the guidebook.) I pack up, then fill my water bottles in a nearby spring, which is a good thing, since the only other water source today (I later find out) is a murky creek six hours from here.

After lunch, I reach the halfway point on the PCT: Mile 1325. I'm hot, thirsty, and a bit incredulous that after walking all this way, I still have just as many miles ahead of me! At some point, I'll have to start paying closer attention to daily mileage in order to make sure that I finish by the end of September.

The weight of my pack is burdensome. It's heavy and awkward. I can't get comfortable. If I get rid of some things I'll be able to walk faster. After a 28-mile day, I hitch into the town of Chester. I'll find the post office tomorrow and send what I don't need home.

The nice hotel in town is full. I stay at the seedy one. At the grocery store, I buy some cough medicine to knock me out so I can sleep in the gross little room. The next day I whittle my gear down to just about nothing, sending one package home and bouncing another 350 miles up trail to Ashland, Oregon. The Ashland package has my tent, stove, windpants, gloves, and a few other items. I want my final days in California to be light, happy, fast ones. With a lot less stuff, the weight of my pack, including food, weights a mere 16 pounds. Sweet. Before leaving Chester, I send an email home.

Hi Everyone,

I hope this finds you well and enjoying a wonderful summer! I'm writing this from the Chester, California Community Center, where there's no wait, no time limit, and no charge for using the Internet. A rare combination! Things are good on the trail. The tricky thing these days is the heat. It's not the dry desert heat like the first 700 miles of this journey. It's more like home: humid and sticky. Given my roots, you'd think I'd be prepared for it, but I'm not!

It's mind-boggling to think I've been walking for over three months. The trail is as much an emotional workout as a physical one, and from its vantage it's easy to watch the internal emotional drift. The simplest things make me extraordinarily happy: a flower, clean water to drink, kindness from another hiker, not being lost. I'm tired and often hungry, but my legs feel strong and I never tire of looking at the sky. By day it's always a deep rich blue and by night filled with shining stars or a fat glowing moon. Sometimes the wide-open western landscape feels infinite, huge, and distant. Other times, the very same landscape, feels shockingly intimate, as if it's part of me, as if it's seeped into my body and we're walking as one. Breathing as one. Often it feels as if I've known no other world, no other way of life. Then I hike out of the woods and into a town and see something that knocks me right back into the person I used to be. For example, petunias. Every time I see them, they catch me off guard. One glance and they jolt me straight back home to the people I know and love. To the New England landscape that pulses through my veins, to corn-on-the-cob and the sea.

On days that I walk alone (nearly all) and I feel like having company, I pick one of you to walk with me. Often, too, I think of Mom—usually when I see her favorite color blue. Blue flowers. Blue butterflies. Blue birds.

Ok. I must get back out there. I'm hoping to make it to Ashland, Oregon in two and a half weeks, if I can.

Thank you for walking this long trail with me.

xoxo, Anne

July 28

I leave the Community Center and hitch as I walk down the road. A car stops and the young man behind the wheel is clean-shaven and congenial. I get in and after a few minutes notice that this nice young man reeks of alcohol. We weave up the road as he tells me about the rock concert he's going to tonight. We're only going nine miles. I grip onto the seat, bide my time, and arrive at the trailhead just fine.

It's 4:00. My plan is to walk 18 miles to a small resort located inside Lassen National Park, called Drakesbad. I add instant coffee to my water bottle, along with cream, a luxury scored at the café I had breakfast at this morning.

The trail rolls gently through a forest and when the sun goes down, all is black. Occasionally, moonlight breaks through a canopy of tree limbs, sending soft rays of light onto the forest floor. It's a lovely walk. I see no one and move at a good clip. My pack feels perfect! Pack light, travel light, and be happy! My new motto!

After six hours of walking, a ghostly figure floats toward me and my heart skips a beat! Am I hallucinating? I pause, and notice the volcanic pool the vapor is rising from. Then I remember the park is called Lassen *Volcanic* National Park. Perhaps I should look at my guidebook more often. There are lights on the other side of a meadow, I pass the volcanic pool and head toward them. I can't find the campground, so camp on the edge of a meadow. It's a very cold night. I bounced my tent to Ashland but kept the fly, poles, and ground cloth. I attach the poles to the ground cloth, then slip the fly over the poles. The fly doesn't reach the ground. While I sleep a steady draft blows in from all four sides. I spend the night shivering. Will I freeze every night for the next three hundred and thirty miles?

Early the next morning, I walk into an empty dining room at the Drakesbad. On each table is a red-checkered tablecloth with a vase of daisies. Vapor from the hot springs pool dances outside the window. A tall man with a handlebar moustache appears in the dining room. He has a friendly smile and a thick Austrian accent: "Goot morning, goot morning! How are you? Vould you like to take a bath?" Music to my ears! I nod and he hands me a towel. After the soak, I have breakfast on the patio with six other hikers. Guests at surrounding tables ask us a lot of questions, and we drink up the attention, along with the excellent coffee.

The seven of us return to the trail and play leapfrog all day, and arrive in the town of Old Station at 6:00. I have a heck of a time finding a good place to camp. Nothing suits me. Either the potential site is too close to the road, too close to the trail, or too close to a house. I give up. Sometimes the perfect campsite just has to wait. I place my ground cloth on earth riddled with 3-inch diameter holes. Snake holes? Will they slither out at night, slide through the drafty gap, and into my space? Whatever. I eat some cheese and crackers, and call it a day.

July 30

The heat is unbearable. I walk beside an alluring river and fall prey to its charms. I spend the whole day beside it: organizing, rinsing out clothes, and reading. At 5:00 I put on my iPod and hike toward Hat Rim. I listen to a Ron Carlson short story and a discussion about Stieg Larsson's life (author of *The Girl with the Dragon Tattoo*). It keeps my mind occupied until I finish the climb. At the top of the rim, a dozen cows awash in a purple sunset glow stare me down. They stand perfectly still with their black eyes bulging.

I walk fast in the fading light, passing a few hikers camped near the trail and a few more camped beside a fire tower, one of whom tells me that he just saw a rattler. I hike a few more miles, then cowboy camp behind bushes, near a dirt road. A car approaches. I hurriedly get inside my sleeping bag, and rest my head on my pack. Did the car pull over? It must have, because now I hear voices. I don't want to be discovered. I remain motionless, listening to a steady stream of muffled voices. Adrenalin courses though my body. What are they doing? Why are they here? When are they going to leave?

My imagination creates a variety of gruesome scenarios. Ten

minutes later, my iPod slips from behind my head. I must have accidentally pressed the play button when I leaned onto my pack. There are no strange people. No car. The muffled voices were from my iPod. All is well.

I didn't walk far today, maybe 12 miles.

July 31

I'm in a pace line with five other hikers; it reminds me of drafting on a bicycle. The person in front sets the pace and the rest of us follow until she drops to the back of the line, and the next person leads for awhile, and so on down the line. The miles fly by. After lunch, we take a dip in a creek near a utility plant, though not without hesitation. Toxins? Hope not. We try not to swallow. After the swim, we split up.

It's dark when I arrive at the Burney Falls State Park Store to pick up the package that's waiting for me. Then I set off in search of a shower. A ranger asks if I'd like a ride to the backpacker's campsite? She drives through a full campground of happy-looking family campers, to the very back. She stops the car, points her index finger toward the dark woods, and says, "Go down that dirt road until you reach the pioneer cemetery. You can't miss it. You'll see the headstones. You can stay there tonight, and you'll have it all to yourself. Free of charge." When she leaves, I find the showers and wash up, then walk back to the park entrance. I declare a patch of grass by the sidewalk home for the night. Not perfect, but it will do. It's almost midnight. I'll get up at the crack of dawn and be out of here before anyone sees me. I open a box of homemade Hungarian cookies sent to me all the way from Connecticut, and by the light of the big bright moon, I gratefully eat every fruity, nutty, crumb.

August 1

Today is the first day of August, which means I have two months to hike 1,240 miles. I do the math: 620 miles per month equals 155 miles per week, which equals 22 miles a day with no days off from now until Canada. But wait! There are 31 days in August and 30 days in September. I have eight weeks plus five days. All I have to do is hike 20.3 miles a day with no days off for 61 days. But I want to take a day off here and there. And what will the terrain be like in Oregon and Washington? Will I be able to hike 20-plus miles in Washington? And thus begins, "The Mileage Game." My mind spins as I crunch and re-crunch numbers. When I've gotten myself sufficiently freaked-out, I decide to focus on only today. I'll take it one day at a time and do the math when I get to Oregon.

The trail is lovely until I hit a stretch where hundreds of trees have been chopped. I walk until a healthy forest returns, stopping when the sky is streaked in orange-red-purple light.

I knocked off 25 easy miles today.

August 2

I'm camped on a knoll just past Butcherknife Creek, sharing the campsite with Appleface, the guy who found my camera in the desert. He's in his tent. I'm sleeping under the stars. Our site is on a steep incline a few yards from the trail. I'm concerned that my restlessness will disturb him and try not to move, but can't help it. I stretch this way and that, sliding downhill a little bit each time, until I've slid all the way to the trail. I crawl back up, re-group, and tell myself not to move. I squirm and slide down the hill again. I make a dam with my gear to keep me in place, a technique perfected weeks ago. This helps, and I sleep.

August 3

5 a.m. is a great time of day to hike! I should do this more often! Mt. Shasta sits firmly on the eastern horizon. She's been following me for days.

I take a long afternoon break, then walk late into the night and camp on a high, flat piece of soft dirt, five miles from the town of Castella.

August 4

At the gas station in Castella, I buy Appleface a long overdue beer. I spend the day resting in the shade. When it's time to go, I follow the trail through Castle Crags State Park until I'm at the base of a steep rocky ridge, laced with dozens of switchbacks. My goal is to make it to the top of the ridge by sunset, but halfway up it starts to get dark. Way back in June the days felt endless, now they feel strangely compressed and dusk always catches me off guard.

On the elbow of a switchback there's just enough room to toss down my sleeping bag. It's an odd place to camp but I doubt anyone will come up here tonight. I roll out my bag and get comfy, then notice a squeaky murmur coming from the rocks beyond my feet. I get up to check it out. Nestled below the switchback, four sets of yellow eyes stare up at me. It's dark, and I can't make out what they are, huddling together on the ledge. They're the size of small kittens. Who's your mama? And where is she? Are you raccoons? No, not up here. Marmots? Doubt it. Mountain lions? Well, you do look rather cat-like. I consider my options: 1) Leave. 2) Set up the fly so mama doesn't step on me if she comes home. 3) Chill out and continue sleeping under the stars.

I choose Option 2. Then gather rocks to place on the edge of the fly. I don't want any animals to crawl inside. It's a feeble attempt. The gap is too wide, but at least I'm making a statement.

Switchback Camp

August 5

I'm walking through a long curvaceous canyon, richly layered in earth tones. The muted colors meld together in a sensuous swath of every possible shade of brown, red, tan, and gold. What's not to love about the Marble Mountains? I feel light in my body, light in my heart, and by the end of the day, I'm 25 miles closer to Oregon.

I stop for the night at 7,600', among patches of snow. I have a view of Mt. Shasta to the east. Though with Shasta, I always feel like it's more about the mountain watching me, than me watching it. Shasta has eyes, heart, and soul. To the south and west, mountains ripple endlessly in front of me. I want to appreciate every inch of what's left in Northern California, especially now that the landscape is spectacular again. But Oregon is very much on my mind. It's only 136 miles from here. I should be there in less than a week.

Omnipresent Mt. Shasta

August 6

While visiting the "ladies room" this morning I leaned my hiking pole against a tree, and when I left, forgot to grab it. I didn't realize this for several miles and chose not to go back for it. I hope someone finds it and get some use out of it.

Today the earth was green, luscious, and bursting with wildflowers! I'm spending the night near a road with Jackal Jim and Appleface. There's an RV parked nearby and two older couples are grilling steaks. Jackal Jim can be a sour-tempered son-of-a-gun when he's hungry and he's almost out of food (as are we). Desperate for a good meal, he digs deep within himself, pulls out a gracious veneer and puts it on. Then he wanders over. They laugh and talk, but he returns crabbier than before he left, having scored only a bottle of water.

August 7

I'm walking with a bunch of PCTers through a meadow filled with thousands of wildflowers. The large group splits into smaller ones, and by early evening I'm alone again. I want to get as close as possible to the town of Etna, 15 miles away. I pass Jackal Jim and A-face camped on the side of a cliff, and consider changing my plans. I'm mulling over this decision, when a loud gaseous outbreak (seismic) erupts from one of the tents. I keep walking.

The only thing I have left to eat is a package of hot chocolate. I rip it open and lick the chalky powder as I walk. Who knew hot chocolate had so much salt? Eating it this way, it's definitely noticeable. A part of me is totally grossed out, but the sugar and salt give me the pep I need to hike until 11:00.

Today was my longest day yet: 34 miles

August 8

I walk six miles on an empty stomach and then hitch into Etna. I find a clean motel room with a spotless bathroom. The owners offer to launder my clothes, which is a huge gift. I eat and sleep well. The next day I get a ride back to the trail with a local who's sipping on a micro-brew. He offers me one and I'm tempted, but decide the bottle will be too much of a hassle to carry. On the entire trail I drink a total of two beers. I climb nine miles to a windy ridge with a stunning view of purple mountains, and spend the night.

High Camp on Ridge

August 10

The trail dips into a meadow where chunks of granite have fallen from the cliffs above. They look like priceless sculptures placed delicately in a fairy garden. I look up to the sky and see something very strange. I can't believe my eyes! For the first time in months it's not blue! The last time the sky was gray was way back at Rae Lake, in the Sierras. Surely, this is evidence that Oregon is near. This thought, along with the cooler temperature, invigorates me. I meet three strong women in their sixties—day hikers—they tell me they've just seen a bear. That's exciting!

I have excellent food with me today, plus I had great food in town. My body is well fueled. I walk strong all day, stopping in the afternoon for a long break, and to eat ramen noodles. They've been soaking in the side pocket of my pack, in a water-filled baggie. This method of cooking works like a crock-pot without the pot. I dump the water out, add avocado, curry, green onions, and eat it straight of the bag. I have coffee, and then hit the trail.

At twilight I meet a young couple, they tell me Girder Creek Campground is 10 miles away. I set my sights on it and kick into high gear. The last few miles are challenging because the trail twists and turns inside a tight, narrow ravine, and it's a very black night. Even in the dark the vegetation looks less Californian and more Oregonian. After a very long time, I cross several bridges and find the campground.

I walked nonstop (except for one brief chat) since 4:30. It's almost midnight. I set my pack down, and prepare a picnic table bed. I get into my bag, but my body can't relax, it wants to keep moving—my muscles twitch and my mind races, until finally, I sleep.

I hiked 41 miles today. (My longest day on the PCT.)

August 11

Seiad Valley is the last town before Oregon. I leave the campground and walk east on the south side of a river for a few miles, then cross a bridge, and road walk west on the north side of the river for a few miles. There may have been a place to ford, but I didn't see it. I spend the afternoon in Seiad Valley, avoiding the heat, and leave at 6 p.m. I have no trouble finding the trail because the PCT blaze near the road is by far the largest blaze I've ever seen. It must be at least three times the size of my head. Clarity is a wonderful thing.

I have only 37 miles left to hike in this state. After a few hot, sweaty, steep miles, I stop for the day. While sleeping, hundreds of little red ants invade my camp. Some of them march their way into my bag, onto my body, and sting. Thank goodness I'll get my tent back in Ashland. It's been an interesting experiment to be without it, but I prefer sleeping in my tent.

August 12

I'm camped seven miles from the Oregon border. This is my last night in California. Wa-hoo! I'm on the edge of a field, hoping to catch a meteor shower that's predicted for tonight. It's cold. I've secured the fly with rocks (sort of) to keep the cool air from blowing onto my face.

Ode to California

I bow a sacred good-bye and good riddance to the state that has brought me thus far. It lives in me now. I have granite elbows and a watery heart and meadowlarks for lungs. My nose is composed of river pebbles. My liver's a high-flying hawk. My abdomen dances with cacti and bear, good-bye California, good-bye. There's no forgetting you now. Your brilliant blue skies, your mountains, your lakes, or the day I was snapped so fully awake (and almost in two) by a creek that flushed out what I already knew: I want to live, I want to live, *I want to really live*—fully awake, fully alive. Good-bye California good-bye.

5

Oregon

State Line

August 13

Friday Morning

I wander up a gentle hill to a discreet wooden sign nailed onto a tree. It reads: Oregon / California. I'm here. I celebrate my arrival by eating an orange that I've somehow managed to hang onto for 60 miles. When that's gone, all I have left are four honey sticks and a few tablespoons of peanut butter to get me to Ashland, which is 27 trail miles and a 13 mile hitch away.

Oregon feels different. I've just crossed the border, but already the earth is softer and greener. Mt. Shasta, 70 miles to the southeast, is still within view, or more correctly, Mt. Shasta's powerful gaze is still on me. I don't understand that serene, powerful mountain. She's everywhere, always. How much longer will she walk with me?

O'Regan in Oregon!

I spend the afternoon walking up and down rolling landscape, hoping to reach Mt. Ashland Campground before dark. It's an easy walk, but by late afternoon I'm famished and my energy is extremely low. I drag myself to the top of a hill and notice a red cooler atop the next one. Is this wishful thinking or could it be trail magic? I pick up the pace, eager to find out. My wish is granted: it's trail magic! I open the lid and stare down upon dozens of empty soda cans, then paw through the sticky mess and find exactly one full can of soda left. I'm the luckiest person on the planet! I've just been gifted calories, hydration, and caffeine! Hurray! The sun sets while the sugary drink recharges my system, and I happily start hiking again.

I arrive at the dirt road where I should take a left to get to the campground. There's loud music coming from that direction, and someone is shouting into a microphone. I can't make out the words. Is it a Friday night rock concert? Or kids hanging out, blasting car stereos? It's been a long day. I want to stop, but know I won't be able to sleep in a noisy campground, so keep walking. I'll camp on the next level piece of earth that I find.

The trail drops into dark woods, the music and shouting are above me now. I come to a wide, open field and start to cross it. Suddenly a floodlight lands on me! Holy cow, what's going on? The light shines from above, where all commotion is. I tuck my chin to my chest and walk as fast as I can. The floodlight tracks my every move. It follows me across the field, until I slip into the dark woods again. What was that all about? There's no way I'm camping anywhere near here now. I've already hiked 25 miles today and not a single cell in my body wants to move another inch, but I have to get away from here. At least by walking a few more miles it will get me closer to Ashland and further away from this strangeness.

At 10:00 I arrive at a swank little inn just a few yards from the trail. It's festooned with tiny white lights on railings and roof, creating the perfect ambiance for the well-heeled crowd that's laughing and flirting on the deck, goblets of wine in-hand. I'm not the least bit prepared for this appealing scene and am overcome with desire for that life, not this. I want to sip chardonnay and eat flakey bits of salmon grilled to perfection. I want to wear a sexy black dress bought this afternoon at a snappy boutique in the hip section of town. I want painted nails and shiny hair and makeup that brings out the blue in my eyes. I want to dab perfume on the back of my neck and imagine falling in love.

I'm a stark, grimy, tired, hungry contrast to all that, and head toward the picnic table on the other side of the inn, all the while hoping no one sees me. The guidebook mentioned that there was a picnic table here. My earlier anticipation of making it my bed for the night seems utterly absurd. I've walked 28 miles with very little food, and for the second time tonight I don't want to take another step. I consider getting a room at the inn but can't fathom mingling with that lovely scene, looking as I do. I leave, walking until I can no longer hear the tinkle of glass, and the rupture of laughter, and flop myself down beside a tall leafy tree. I roll out my sleeping and get in. Closing my eyes, I remind myself that I've made it all the way to Oregon. And that thought puts everything right.

August 14

I get up at dawn and walk along the edge of a narrow canyon. I glance to my right and floating eye-level, practically close enough to touch (well, close enough to hit with a baseball maybe) is a blimp! It silently drifts like a huge, dark whale in an ocean of air. What kind of magical curious place is this? Oregon, we're off to an interesting start!

I make my way to the Interstate 5 on-ramp and stick my thumb up toward the bright morning sun. It's Saturday and traffic is thin. I notice a scruffy-looking thru-hiker coming down from the trail. As he gets closer, I realize it's Coyote Joe. He's a physical therapist from Georgia. If you don't know him, the first time you lay eyes on him the term "escaped convict" might come to mind. He has long red hair, a straggly beard, and beady little eyes. He's a serious fellow with a grim demeanor and a scowling face. Whenever I see him he's always struggling with something: his too-tight shoes, the blistering heat, not finding water. We all struggle with these things but he deals with it differently. He expresses his frustrations in an over-the-top, cartoon-ish way that makes me smile.

As soon as I see him I think, "Please just wave and go to the motel down the road. Better yet, don't even notice me, don't even wave—just keep walking. If you do notice me and come over, please don't ask to hitch with me. Just keep walkin' m'friend. Just keep walkin'."

If he joins me, we'll never get a ride. I know he's a great guy but it's impossible for a stranger driving on the highway to know this. I'm hungry beyond belief and want to get into town *asap*. "Please keep walking Coyote. Please keep walking…"

"*Hey Anne!*" he shouts. "*Mind if I hitch with you?*"

An hour later, we're still standing there when he growls, "Want to split a cab into town?" I do not. A half hour later, we get a ride. This is the longest hitch on the entire trail for me. As we squish ourselves into the back seat of the dark blue Toyota Corolla that has stopped for us, Coyote whispers, "Wow, this is the fastest hitch I've ever had."

We're dropped off at the edge of town, find a motel, register for rooms, and have breakfast together. The food at the nearby diner is fabulous. Over blueberry pancakes I get to know Coyote—a true gem of a guy—even better. He tells me about his family, his work, and his life growing up in the south.

August 15

Ashland is great. I keep thinking, "I could live here. I could *really* live here." There are fantastic restaurants, an annual Shakespeare

Festival, mountain shops, gorgeous flowers, sweet homes, a food co-op, and a deeply discounted natural food store. The post office is closed on Saturday so I'm stuck here until Monday. I'd rather be hiking, but if I've got to be stuck in a town for a few days, I can't think of a better one!

The natural food store with the great deals sells every organic product you can imagine: food, produce, shampoo, lotion, soap. And it happens to be located across the street from my motel. I go there four times. It's my kind of store. The peanut butter that I like usually costs $1.20 per individually wrapped package, here they're on sale for a quarter! I stock up on them and many other items. I have to mail food to Oregon and Washington. I prepared my California drops from home, but waited until Ashland to put together drops for Oregon and Washington, because who knew if I'd make it this far? I'm elated that I have such fabulous food options to choose from here.

On Sunday night, an epic thunderstorm rips through town. Heavy rain floods the motel parking lot. One-by-one, doors swing open and hikers step outside their rooms to gape at the storm. We flash knowing looks at each other as we watch thick bolts of lightening splice through the sky, zapping the mountains we'll soon be walking in. We're witnessing something we haven't seen much of in the past three months: weather! I shiver to think of what the next 1,000 miles will bring.

August 16

It's extremely hot and humid standing by the side of the road with my thumb thrust into the dense air, waiting for a ride back to the trail. Rays of sun impale me as I wait and wait. This might be the hottest day yet.

At a coffee shop this morning, there was a flyer taped to the window. It advertised a religious revival held at the Mt. Ashland Campground the night the floodlight tracked me. I guess someone just wanted to "spread the light."

A car stops and gives me a ride. When I get out, I walk two miles up a quiet road to the trail. I've been off-trail for three days but it feels much longer. Though it doesn't take long to ease myself back into this earthy world. After hiking four trail miles, I camp on a hillside. I'm ecstatic to have my tent back. Aside from keeping bugs and weather out, it also provides me with a sense of security. I've missed that, and will sleep easier now. I'm camped on a slant and strategically place my pack beneath my sleeping mat, to even things out, a strategy used many times by now. I watch as the red-hot day cools to a golden simmer. Night descends, stars appear. I'm home once again.

August 17
I hiked 29 miles today. The sunset was a streaky, orange-purple light mixed with low diaphanous clouds and thin mist. The Oregon woods are very dark at night. I'm camped near a big rock beside an empty narrow dirt road.

August 18
A few words about guidebooks.

Guidebook #1 – written by Mr. Negative
While I planning the hike at home, I learned some useful things from this book. However, on the trail it's not very helpful because information that I need in a hurry, like, "where do I go from here?" is buried deep inside wordy text. Also, it seems the author was in a foul mood when he wrote the book. Example: "Look to

the west. The trail meanders through an unattractive valley then crosses an alder-choked stream before arriving at more dull scenery. If only the trail went up over that peak to the east (land dispute, maybe someday it will) then you'd have a stellar view and an incredible hiking experience. But for now you're stuck with this." I dumped this book in southern California.

Guidebook #2 – written by Ms. Glass is Always Full
This book is a good resource for town information and also offers useful trail tips. It was written by an optimistic thru-hiker. I like this guide but some hikers find it too optimistic.

Guidebook #3 – written by Mr. Made It Up
It's cool because this book has lots two-color elevation graphs. But everyone gripes about it because it's chock full of inaccuracies.

When I stopped at a cabin today, I read an entry in a logbook that sums up the tone of each guidebook pretty well:

Book #1: Oregon is all uphill and has no water.
Book #2: Oregon is all downhill and has plenty of water.
Book #3: The trail does not go through Oregon.

The most valuable guides for me have been Benjamin Go's, *PCT Data Book*, and *The Water Report* (for the desert), available on the PCTA website. I wish I'd known about Half-Mile's maps (free on the internet), everybody raves about them.

August 20
The full moon rises above Crater Lake. Its lunar light shimmers onto the water below, as I walk the perimeter of the crater. The wind is howling like crazy. There's a cluster of dwarf pines across

the road. I decide to check them out, and once among them, see an appealing spot that would make a perfect hideout. I pitch my tent and get comfy, pressing my back against the volcanic earth, as I watch the night sky. I can't sleep. My body is highly charged and my mind keenly alert. A car drives by on the distant horizon. I follow the headlights until they disappear. The earth feels seismically alive; molecules seem to be dancing wildly beneath my body, leaping into the tent, and seeping into my pores. Everything feels radically different camped in this windy, wild place. I spend the entire night wide-awake when I should be sleeping...

Volcano Camp

August 21

I take a nap after lunch. When I wake, I do the math. I've been hiking whatever distance I want each day, usually high mileage but not always. I haven't felt pressured to hike only 20-plus days, nor have I felt the need to avoid going into towns in order to make better time. The math tells me that the jig is up. If I want reach Canada before it snows—before September 30th—I need to walk at least 25 miles a day, every day, from now on. I've been on the trail for almost four months. I'm healthy and my legs feel like steel. Hiking in Oregon has been fast and easy so far, but what about the rest of the state? And what about Washington? Will the mountains in Washington be challenging? The only thing I know for sure is that I need to get to Canada before the snow. The pressure is on.

Crater Lake

A few miles later, I meet a thru-hiker sitting on a log. She has a case of the blues. Apparently she's been doing the math, too. She says she wishes the PCT were like the Appalachian Trail. She hiked the AT southbound and there was no need to hurry, because there was no snow to beat. She was able to savor her last few weeks by walking just a few miles a day, and yearns to do the same thing now. I totally get it. The thought of having to hike 25-miles every day for the next 40 days is daunting.

I adore Oregon. I've been here eight days (the first three in town) and have been surprised each day—by a blimp, by wildflowers, by crazy sunsets, and by oddly beautiful Crater Lake. Tonight I'm camped beside a creek a few miles below Mt. Thielson, the tip of which is covered in fog. This landscape reminds me of bear country: gnarly mountains, lush meadows, clear creeks. I've only seen one bear on the trail and that was way back in June, but I sense they may be nearby.

I eat a skimpy dinner of organic ramen and figs. I can't believe I'm almost out of food again. *Is this even possible?* Unfortunately, it is.

August 22

I hiked 30 miles today, which means I have 5 miles in the bank. I'm camped atop a sandy hill. Luckily, late this afternoon I met a Trail Angel. He's done the PCT twice, once in 1976 and again 2007. He comes to the trail two weekends every August, with food for hikers. I was out of food and water when I saw his yellow Volkswagen parked at a trail junction. It was the perfect place to "Angel." He encouraged me to eat as much as I could, because he was heading home in an hour. I took him up on his kind offer and ate the following: 4 yodels (calories!), a cinnamon raisin bagel smothered with cream cheese, another one stuffed with turkey, mayo, and avocado, chocolate covered graham crackers, a soda, and lots of water. I took a yogurt and an apple to go, which I just ate. The apple was pure heaven—crispy, juicy, sublime. I'm not sure how I would've pushed myself another 10 miles today, or into Shelter Cove tomorrow, without a boost from all that food.

I must, must, must, must, must carry enough food for the next section of trail and try hard not to eat it all in the first two days.

August 23

My air mattress leaks. Last night it held air for an hour, and then went flat. I blew it up and an hour later, my body pressed into cold sand. I blew it up every hour until dawn. At Shelter Cove (a tiny resort with a small store, a few cabins, and a gorgeous lake), I mention my predicament to Roundabout. He's leaving to go back to work and kindly offers me his air mattress. I buy food, get on the trail, and after seven miles (plus eight this morning) I make camp by a lovely lake. I sit on Roundabout's air mattress and a feeling of dread sweeps over me. It's not insulated. Visions of my first week on the trail when I froze every night, come to mind. It's almost midnight, and I'm too cold to sleep.

August 25

Last night I slept on pine boughs that I ripped from downed trees. It was awful. It wasn't comfortable, or warm. Though it did smell good. This morning I walked to Elk Lake Resort and caught a ride into Bend. I went to REI and bought a new mat. I'm spending tonight at Roundabout's house. He'll drive me back to the trail early tomorrow morning. Bend seems like a nice place!

August 26

I walked 31 miles today, loving every minute, every moment, every mountain, every inch of this peculiar place. The trail skirted alongside Mt. Jefferson, and beside Obsidian Falls, then meandered beneath colorful petrified cliffs, and through a narrow ravine. Wispy clouds clung to twisted, rocky, red-brown spires. Late in the day I smelled smoke. In Bend, I was told there's a fire somewhere up the trail. I come to a wide expanse of black lava beds, turn right, and set up camp at Lava Lake. Oregon keeps gifting me with one enchantment after another.

Lava bed

It's impossible to describe strange beauty... an obsidian path leading to a waterfall that whispers, whispers, whispers. Crumbling, mineral-laced mountains with scaly, glittering, skin... like fish heads pointing toward heaven, gasping for air... grasping for god... reaching for reason and ancient understandings... yours, mine... a turbulent fiery earth, now black and scratchy, stretching for miles... black against cobalt blue, my new horizon... four billion years woven inside one moment, one instant, one breath... one single stride.

August 27
Today is Mom's birthday.

Doris Elizabeth Church O'Regan
August 27, 1919 – May 5, 2010

Cinco de Mayo (excerpt)
By Naomi Shihab Nye, TRANSFER

If this is your birthday and you are dead,
do we stay silent as the sheet
you died under? No. You always talked.
Here's a thick white candle whispering.
Pour birdseed into feeders.
Speak up, speak up.

August 29
I am a student of rain. It's been pouring nonstop for two whole days. The sound of it on my tent is lovely. There, I've said something pleasant. Oh, and since it's too raw, wet, and cold to stop during the day, it's easy to tick off high-mileage days. I hiked two 30-milers in a row. That's two pleasant thoughts. Now for the rest of the story.

This morning I do something I was hoping to avoid: I slip out of my warm, dry sleeping bag and into sopping wet clothes. Damp, cold cloth clings to my body, sending chills throughout my entire being. I hurriedly gather my gear. In a few days, when I reach

Cascade Locks, I'll pick up my windpants. They have a thin fleece lining which should help keep me warm even when wet.

The trail is covered with elderberry bushes. For the next two hours, whenever I touch a branch, it showers me with cold water. I come to a sign stating that the trail is closed due to the (smoldering) fire. The detour takes me to a parking lot where a ranger is waiting to give me a ride, thus eliminating a 25-mile road walk. I miss eight miles of the PCT because of the fire, but am grateful for the ride. As we drive along, we pass a hiker I met yesterday named Lily. The ranger says she didn't want a ride. We're on a narrow road with speeding cars. I don't envy her decision. Lily's an attorney. There are a few attorneys on the trail this year, re-thinking their careers. When I saw Lily yesterday she was miserable because her gear was soaked. (A week later she drops off the trail, a hard decision when you've made it this far.)

The ranger who gives me my second ride (i.e. first ranger calls second ranger to transfer cargo—me) is a woman in her thirties who used to live in Manhattan. When she drops me off, the sun makes a brief appearance. I pull everything out of my pack and spread it around, willing it will dry. An hour later, thick black clouds roll in and I move on. I pass a large pond and then enter an Indian reservation, assuming I'll see some sign of human life. But all I see is woods and rain. I find a patch of mud to camp on, and call it a day.

August 30

It was too rainy to stop for more than a few minutes today, therefore, I managed to knock off 35 miles. Even with all those miles, I didn't see a single person. It was easy hiking except for the rain, and I would've walked further if I hadn't lost the trail in the dark. I'll find it tomorrow.

My tent is pitched just inches from the trail. I don't think anyone will walk by at this late hour. I hope the sharp rocks beneath my tent don't pop my new air mattress. My ground cloth is thick and I put clothes under my mat for padding. I think I'll be ok. I'm at Mile 2101 and will be out of Oregon in a day or two.

This afternoon I got a few glimpses of Mt. Hood. A miracle of a mountain! Her snowy, jagged peak was wrapped in a shroud of drifting vapor. I didn't see much of her but what I did see took my breath away. I've changed her name from Mt. Hood to Mt. Miraculous! She's quite possibly the most beautiful mountain I've ever seen.

Mt. Hood

August 31

I'm walking as fast as I can, trying to get to Timberline Lodge in time for the breakfast buffet. I'm daydreaming about waffles when I look up and see a bear cub in front of me! Nothing like an early morning encounter with a bear to snap a girl back into the present moment. *"Hey bear—hey bear—hey little guy!"* It takes off. Mama bear, are you around?

After a few more miles, the firm earth morphs into a sandy path, then the sandy path turns into a sand dune. I feel like I'm on Cape Cod. Honestly, Oregon! You amaze me. I only get to have one more day with you before reaching Washington. I miss you already.

To my extreme joy, the restaurant is open when I arrive. The elegant dining room is replete with tablecloths, silver trays, and china. Yet no one seems to mind grubby hikers. I blissfully eat waffles, crepes, omelets, fruit, coffee, and juice. When I step back outside, the weather is nasty. A hard monsoon-like rain pounds down and an intense wind blows. I fall prey to the charms of the beautifully restored lodge and book a room. All day and all night the wind howls, while the rain beats against my window.

September 1

After another satisfying breakfast at the lodge I get on the trail and a short while later arrive at the Zigzag River. It's running high and fast from last night's rain and it takes me quite a while to find a good place to cross. I meet a German guy on the other side and we hike together for the rest of morning. At dusk, I take the turnoff for Salvation Springs and follow the path down to a muddy trickle of water. My camp is low and damp and surrounded by thick bushes and tall creepy trees. If I let myself, I could get spooked down here. But why bother?

September 2

I walk by Eagle Creek, then into the small town of Cascade Locks, which is situated on the banks of the Colombia River. Washington is on the opposite shore. I watch a barge loaded with logs float down the river. Behind my camp, trains chug along, shaking the earth as they come and go.

At the grocery store I'm assaulted by an awful smell that intensifies as I walk down the aisle. In fact, it's so strong I have to cover my nose. At the end of the aisle, I take a left and bump into the source of this powerful stench. A hiker. As we chat, I have Dali-like visions of clocks warping, paint peeling, and milk curdling in reaction to his powerful scent. We say good-bye and he flashes me a big toothy grin. Yep, he's one of my peeps. Later I see him at the campground rinsing his clothes in an outdoor sink. He triumphantly announces that he hasn't used a washing machine since the Mexican border.

I spend a restless night listening to trains. But at least it's not raining, plus the soft earth is extremely comfortable. I'm one night away from reaching the third and final state of this long hike north. Life is very good.

6

Washington

Labor Day Weekend

The Bridge of the Gods was built by the devil. It dangles high above the Columbia River, connecting Oregon to Washington. I step onto the narrow, open-grate steel (no sidewalks), and glance down past my toes to the river. Fumes from the bumper-to-bumper traffic waft through the air. I feel sick. I turn to look down-river, and my pack grazes the side of a mini-van. The view is lovely: a brilliant blue sky, light dancing on water, green forests lining both banks of the river. I carefully negotiate my way across the bridge and when my feet hit terra firma, the sign I've walked over 2,000 miles to see is before me: "Welcome to Washington."

The broiling sun beats down on me and I hasten my pace. I want to get off this black pavement as soon as possible. I find the trail, and twenty minutes later arrive at a clear-cut forest, where stumpy remains push up from the earth like rotting teeth—a giant earth ache. Standing among this mess it's impossible not to ache, too. *This is Washington?* I walk until I come to a forest and take a campsite beside the path. It's strange to camp so close to the trail, especially because I'm only eight miles from the road. Who might walk by tonight? When I first started thru-hiking two years ago, one mile "in" felt like deep wilderness. These days eight miles "in" feels too close to the road.

The next morning the rocky trail traverses back and forth up the side of a mountain, leading me to a field of golden grass, swaying delicately in a soft breeze. A mile or two later, acres of elderberry bushes laden with ripe fruit appear. I plop berry after berry into my mouth. Their juicy sweetness overwhelms my senses as my purple-stained fingers reach for just one more berry, then another and another. Thus my love affair with the state of Washington begins.

Breakfast!

I feast on berries until forcing myself to leave. A short while later, fluorescent pink tape tied to a branch flutters in the wind. Printed on the tape, in black magic marker, is a large 26. My heart soars, could this mean a trail race? A mile later, more pink tape, this one with a 25 on it, and then the first runner. Yippee! Entertainment! I applaud as the lead runner passes me and for the next several hours

I cheer runners on. At the 13-mile mark, there's an aid station with lots food: chips, chocolate, sandwiches, watermelon and a variety of drinks. The volunteers tell me to eat as much as I want.

It's been four months since my last run, the longest I've gone without running in over three decades! I munch on chips, watching as runners come and go. I yearn to ditch my pack and join them. I watch until the last runner stumbles into the aid station. He's a muscular, older fellow with a shock of white hair, and he's in rough shape. The volunteers tactfully suggest that he might prefer to stay here, rather than continue the race. He's in a stupor and doesn't respond. He eats a peanut butter sandwich, drinks a cup of water, then gets up and staggers away.

This has been a fine way to start my first full day in Washington: elderberries, kindred runner-spirits, and unexpected food! A few miles up the path, I meet a different breed of people. I'm climbing the trail toward a dirt road, when suddenly two men with rifles appear. I ask, "What are you hunting?" "Bear," one of them responds. Up until this point in my life the only kind of hunting I've ever encountered is bargain hunting (which I might add, I excel at). I find this encounter unnerving.

At dusk, I stop at Stabler's Country Store, and then continue on until I reach Panther Creek. The word "panther" gets me thinking about how once I camped near Deer Creek and saw lots of deer, and how once I camped near Bear Creek and saw a bear. I saw a panther (a.k.a. mountain lion, puma, catamount, or cougar) last year while on the Colorado Trail, so figure the odds are low that I'll see another because mountain lion sightings are rare. But just in case, I keep a keen eye out as I prepare dinner. During my first day in Washington, I saw dozens of runners and two hunters but not a single backpacker. As it turns out, throughout the 502 miles of Washington trail, I will see only five other northbound PCTers: two couples and one solo hiker. I do see many more hunters.

September 5
Night hiking has been difficult because of fog. Tonight I walked two hours in a dark, thick, damp haze. I wanted to keep going but couldn't see the narrow trail. I'm camped on a slope and it's raining. I've walked 64 miles in this state and so far it's been a series of long climbs and gradual descents without many views. Elderberries (can't resist) are slowing my pace down considerably.

September 6
At the Trout Lake trailhead, there's a clean, lidded trash barrel filled with healthy snacks donated by the Mt. Adams Zen Center (Trout Lake, WA.) Thank you, Zen Center! I get a ride into town with a couple hauling two horses. They've spent the day riding. They drop me off at a little café, where I have a cup of tea and a bucket of drama. Somehow I manage to lose my passport, credit cards, and cash. Two employees help me turn the place upside down looking for them. After much turmoil, I find them inside my pack and sheepishly call off the search. I meet up with some east coast friends, now transplants to this tiny western town, and sleep on their deck under a bright starry sky.

September 7
After breakfast, my friend Mia drives me to Hood River, Oregon to buy fuel and a new pair of running shoes. I find shoes but the town is out of canister fuel!

In the afternoon, Mia's herb teacher, Kris, visits. We laugh and tell stories as we stir herbal potions. Kris offers me dried cherries for the trail. Mia and her husband Pete gift me with smoked wild salmon, which I eat on the spot, not wanting to tempt bears in the wilderness.

Mia drops me off at the trail at 6:00 p.m., moments later the heavens break loose and it pours. It's pitch dark by seven o'clock these days. I take the first possible campsite that I find, which happens to be atop a layer of sturdy little vines.

September 8

I was extremely uncomfortable last night. No more of this! From now on only flat, comfortable campsites will do! There are two small holes in the side of my tent. Where did they come from? Could an animal have possibly chewed them? I roll up my sleeping bag and notice little black dots on the tent floor that look suspiciously like mouse scat. Is that even possible? Did a mouse chew its way into my tent last night? Nah….

A few miles after breaking camp, I catch a glimpse of regal Mt. Adams poking through a cluster of low-hanging clouds. The sun comes out. I place my wet tent on a slab of granite to dry, and eat a bowl of oatmeal. An hour passes and the rain returns, but an hour is all it takes to dry my tent and damp clothes.

It rains hard until the end of the day when the fat raindrops dissolve into an opaque mist. I find a flat spot under a tall tree for the night. I walked 25 miles today and once again, saw no one. I'm on my knees putting up my tent, when I turn to reach behind me for a stake. Hovering above me are two men dressed in army fatigues. They have black paint smeared on their faces! I scream. Holy cow where did they come from? They're holding weird contraptions in their arms that look like a cross between a musical instrument and a violent one. It takes me a few seconds to realize that they're carrying hi-tech bows and arrows, the likes of which I've never seen before. They apologize for scaring me and proceed to make friendly conversation.

They ask questions about the PCT and tell me a friend of theirs thru-hiked it last year. They're upbeat, and pleasant, and clearly attempting to make me feel comfortable. Which actually makes me feel more uncomfortable. I can't stop thinking they're trying to put me at ease, the way they might attempt to put their prey at ease just before going in for the kill. It strikes me, a woman alone in the woods, and completely unfamiliar with hunting culture, as all very strange. We talk a little more before they silently stalk off into the damp, dark night. Two thru-hikers show up and decide to camp with me. This is the only time I camp with anyone in the entire state of Washington, and their timing could not have been better.

September 9

In the morning, I push my way through chin-high wet bushes and with each step that I take, icy water pours over me. A cold steady stream drips down my pants and into my shoes. After an hour of this, not only am I freezing, but my feet are numb. I stop in a clearing to change out of synthetic socks and back into the dirty, wet wool socks I wore yesterday. My feet begin to thaw, proof that wool really does provide warmth even when wet. It's too rainy and raw to stop again. I keep moving until mid-afternoon, pausing just long enough to heat some hot chocolate and eat a trail bar. I'm getting low on fuel. I savor each sip of the warm chocolate, knowing that liquid warmth may soon not be an option.

By the time I reach Packwood Glacier, a thick fog has set in again. I can't see much but can hear the high-pitched whistle of a marmot as I climb toward a narrow land formation called Knife's Edge. I climb and climb. When the fog dissipates, I gape at the mountainous wilderness surrounding me. Its raw beauty is breathtaking. I can't move. The fog returns and the wind picks up. I move. At the top of Knife's Edge the wind gusts must be at least 60 or 70 mph. The narrow path has steep drops on either side. I round a corner and an orange tent is in front of me. It whips around crazily in the wind. Is this a mirage? Can it really be? I shout "Hello." Two male voices shout "Hello" back. I ask if they're okay, and one of them pokes his head out. He looks about 40, and has short blond hair. He says that he and his friend drove up from Olympia to play in nature for the weekend, but they don't want to hike any further in these conditions. We say good-bye. I continue walking until the ridge is just a few feet wide. With the wind, fog, rain, and steep drop-offs, I'm definitely *not* having a good time. It takes all my focus to keep from falling into the abyss. When a strong gust tips me off balance, I promise the God of All Things that if I get off this mountain alive I'll never, ever, do anything like this again.

The trail splits: one sign says "hikers" and the other "horses." Horses, up here? (Two days later, a local tells me a horse died near this very spot last week.)

Clinging to one rock, then another, I make my way across the ridge and then begin the long down-climb. I walk in the fog until it finally lifts. The rain stops and a plateau appears, layered with pink and purple wildflowers. Waterfalls tumble from lush green cliffs while sparkling streams dance and sing at my toes. Who knew that such exquisite beauty existed? My shoulders relax and my breath returns, as I traipse through a steep valley laced with a string of clear turquoise pools.

I enter a forest and find a damp piece of earth to sleep on for the night, then eagerly fire up my stove for a warm cup of tea. It sputters and dies. I'm officially out of fuel. I have a meager selection of unappealing food in my bag. I skip dinner. All my clothes are wet. With no other choice, I slip into my sleeping bag naked, grateful for its warmth, and fall asleep with my stomach growling. I walked 28 miles today. What a day! Washington is incredible…

September 10

Two hunters pass my by tent before dawn. When they're out of sight, I pack up and hike 11 miles to White's Pass where there's a small café and a dryer by the restroom. I gratefully toss in my wet clothes. After a long break, I get back on the trail and meet more hunters. This time I don't feel quite as uncomfortable. I'm getting used to them. We chat for a bit. I walk five miles and camp on a small hill. The air is damp, the trees are damp, everything is damp, but I'm warm and dry and my belly is full. I have all I need. It's very quiet. And still. I can hear my heart beat.

September 11

When I see Mt Rainier miles away on the western horizon, my tired mind suggests I can touch it if I extend my arm, letting it unravel above the valley of pointed firs that separate us. I'm captivated by its solid, grounded, graceful presence and hope some of its aura will rub off onto me. I need mountains in my life the way some people need chocolate.

I continue walking the rocky trail and splashing through streams. It's that hushed time of day just before dusk when I never see animals, but I sense them preparing for their evening prowl. I imagine cougars lurking ahead near the bend in the trail and bears lumbering toward me from behind. I'm weary and could use a distraction from my overactive imagination so I pull out my iPod. Nothing new here. I've listened to everything at least five times. The only thing I've managed to avoid for the past 2,300 miles is a dharma talk by Pema Chodron. I love Pema but who needs her out here? Certainly, not me.

Mt. Rainier

Who needs a talk on the spiritual life when walking alone for thousands of miles in the wilderness? This long trail has given me lessons she couldn't possibly match; its pushed me, wearied me, worried me, woken me, held me, gifted me many times over, and once nearly stole my life. Who needs Pema? I want lightness and laughter and love—I have no time for her. I'm busy walking ledges eye-to-eye with hawks. I'm busy listening to cedars breath and chasing triple rainbows. This is the world I inhabit now—this is the world I live in day after day, week after week, month after month. Nowadays, I sip pinesap at teatime and munch cloud puffs for lunch, chew beet-red sunsets for dinner and gargle with rocks. How can I possibly listen to Pema?

But I do, I let her speak and she says: "Open yourself to the unknown future with warmth and spaciousness—life is a thrill, not a threat." And I whisper aloud, *"Oh my gosh, she's been here!"* Her words collide with the stones in my bones—with the heat in my blood—with the air in my hair, as I listen, and listen, and listen to her.

An hour passes. I meet a cheese-maker and his wife from Seattle. They give me some homemade Brie, dried fruit, crackers, and almonds. I make camp on the edge of a field covered with purple wildflowers. Chinook Pass is unfurled below me like a long black snake. I take a bite of the precious cheese and it melts in my mouth like a pungent gumdrop. Over and over I hear Pema's words in my mind: *"Open yourself to the unknown future with warmth and spaciousness. Life is thrill, not a threat!"*

September 12

I'm walking through a berry patch, singing at the top of my lungs in order to scare away any hungry bears. I don't meet a bear but I do meet a southbound PCTer named Froggie. His unique approach to the trail is that he drives north and hikes south. He has two cars. He leaves one car at a trailhead and drives the other 50 miles north, then spends the night in a hotel. The next day he hikes 25 miles south to his first car and drives 50 miles north again. He's been hiking 25 miles south, and driving 50 miles north each day since the Mexican border. It must have been challenging to execute this plan in the Sierras and other remote locations. He has a job on the east coast and works from 4:00 a.m. to 1:00 p.m. PST, using hotel wifi. He starts walking each day at 1 p.m., and carries a small daypack. There's more than one way to walk a long trail.

September 13

Froggie told me about a log cabin he passed, and I made it my goal last night. I slept on the front porch. It's the only shelter I've seen on the trail. There were four hikers (in for a week) inside the dark, smoky cabin. It was lovely to have company, but I prefer my wilderness camps.

I leave the shelter at sunrise and find a cooler in the bushes, left behind from a recent mountain bike race. Receiving an unexpected apple and juice is pure bliss. Beyond the cooler is a large burn area where hundreds of thin, silver-scorched trees stand amid red-orange-green undergrowth.

I listen to hunters blowing elk bugles all day. They use them to attract elk. I'm concerned a hunter might see something moving (me) in the woods and think I'm an elk, therefore, whenever it feels too quiet for too long, I sing a chant I learned ages ago: *Om Namo Bhagavate Vasudevaya, Om Namo Bhagavate Vasudevaya...* I sing it over and over and louder and louder, pouring my heart, soul, and nervous energy into each round. I don't want to be mistaken for an elk, plus the chanting soothes me. I camp deep in the woods on a low, flat, moist piece of earth. It's silent down here—*except—* an arrow just whizzed by my tent!

September 14

I meet the northbound-southbound car-hopping hiker again.

Later, when I arrive at Snoqualmie (which means ferocious people) Pass and see the I-90 sign, it reminds me of home. It's the same road that splices through my home state. Interesting how something as simple as an interstate highway sign can make a person feel homesick.

There's a ski area, gas station, and hotel at the pass. The sun has made a rare appearance and I don't want to stop but I need food. And a shower would be nice, so I get a room.

September 15
It's slim pickings at the gas station. My re-supply amounts to ramen, peanuts, and not much else. I'm back on the trail by noon. After a few hours, the landscape shifts from incredibly beautiful to simply outrageous. I walk for 12 miles in a gnarly, misty, undulating, astonishing, natural world. A mountain goat and her kid cross my path and trot up a hillside as soft light spills down from a cloudy sky, first brightening then dimming the earth. I secure my tent on the side of a mountain just moments before the sky turns black, thunder claps, and raindrops heave onto this earthly paradise.

September 16
It rained hard all day in this impossibly beautiful place. I'm inside my tent near the Waptus River and all my gear is soaked except for my sleeping bag, one pair of underwear, and my gloves. May the sun bless these mountains with her presence tomorrow!

September 17
No sun. I walk all day in cold, pelting rain. I see no one in this remote mountainous world. This world, which by now feels like the ultimate secret, and totally mine, is worth every inconvenience.

Waptus River Camp

The last few miles are steep and foggy, as I negotiate my way down a talus field in the dark. When I reach the bottom, I pitch my tent under a tree. It feels like midnight. I check my watch. It's only 8 o'clock. Everything is wet. I'm cold and hungry but okay.

September 18

Last night was long, cold, and supremely uncomfortable. I get up at first light and hike to Steven's Pass (Mile 2476). From here, it's only 174 miles to Canada, though "only" is a relative term. I'm going to Seattle today to visit family, re-group, and pick up a few things: fuel (which I haven't had for 200 miles), a wool shirt, and a new silk liner for my sleeping bag because my current one is in shreds. With the luxury of these few new items, I hope to finish the trail in comfort!

September 20

Seattle was a tremendous gift. It's early afternoon and I just got dropped off at the trail. Now it's time to start walking the final miles to Canada! I throw on my pack and start hiking in light rain, then it begins to storm. I grab my umbrella and pop it open. All my gear is dry and I want to keep it that way. Torrents of rain pound onto the earth and bounce back up onto me. I'm getting rained on from both directions, above and below! This is the heaviest downpour yet.

I see two hikers ahead. As I get closer, I realize that it's Gotcha and her husband Dingo. I'm 320 miles into the state of Washington and this is only the second time I've met northbound hikers. I'm very excited to see them. They're a married couple in their late 30's whom I met in northern California. I catch up to them and we stand in the pouring rain exchanging hellos and then start hiking. It's clear that this is not a temporary rain shower so we stop to adjust gear. I grab a hat, they put on rain pants, and we get moving again, shouting at one another in order to be heard above the pounding rain. Their company is a sweet distraction from these difficult conditions.

We share stories but the sound of rain hitting my umbrella makes it difficult to hear. I don't want to miss a single word and figure since I'm mostly wet anyway, what difference will it make if I put my umbrella away and get my head, back, and shoulders wet too? Inside my pack I have warm dry clothes, wrapped in a thick black trash bag, to change into later. It'll be fine. I put the umbrella away and am instantly soaked, but time passes quickly and happily as we hike along shouting, laughing, and moving as fast as we can to stay warm. We stop briefly to eat hard-boiled eggs that I brought from Seattle and then stop again to find a tree (three trees). A good sign, we're all hydrated. Other than that, we keep moving and hike strong and fast in the near-blinding rain.

I flash back to the Southern Californian desert and to a guy named Tomato. He did the PCT last year and is doing it again this year because he said the rain in Washington had "gotten to him." He said he wants to get it right this time. Way back in the hot, dry desert I had a difficult time imagining what he was talking about. Now I get it. This is what he was talking about: cold rain, wet clothes, wet feet, and no long breaks because it's too cold to stop for more than a moment. This is the difficult side of Washington, this, plus the accumulated physical weariness of having been on the trail for many months and the surprisingly (at least to me) challenging terrain. Who knew Washington had mountains like this?

At the beginning of the PCT, everyone had an edge on about the Sierras. What will they be like in a high snow year? Should you carry an ice ax? What about flipping? Should you push through to Mammoth or re-supply sooner? And what about fording creeks? And on and on… How best to do this in the Sierras? How best to do that? No one spoke about Washington. Washington was a dream too far away to consider. To speak of it felt presumptuous. It was enough to talk about the high mountains that lie on the other side of the long desert we were walking through. To speak of mountains a couple of thousand miles, and several months away, was irrelevant. Who knew if we were really going to make it that far anyway? Talking about it might jinx things.

Washington remained a mystery to me until I got here, and with each step that I take it quietly, richly, dramatically reveals itself. There's nothing subtle about this state. The mountains are rugged and steep, the vegetation is alive in vibrant shades of red, orange, and green; even the weather is dramatic. Washington is the Promised Land, and I've reached it still carrying with me the hopeful promise of touching Canadian soil.

As I walk through the heavy rain with Gotcha and Dingo, I know I'm okay. The weather won't get me today. I'm fresh from town with excellent food in my pack: herbed crackers, nut butters, organic veggies, dried dates, figs, and raisins. I have fuel, which means I can once again have hot coffee in the morning and hot tea at night. Hooray! Life is good. Plus all my clothes are clean, dry and safely tucked away. It's all good. I'm happy to be back on the trail, happy to be with friends, and happy to be only two sections (104 and 78 miles) away from the finish.

We hike for five hours, mostly uphill, until there's a break in the rain. It's six o'clock and too early to stop but I notice a nice flat area set back from the trail under a tree. It's very appealing, and I'll be well prepared for the night if I camp tucked away in this good spot. I say good-bye to my friends and head toward it.

I take my time getting there, clearing a stone here, removing a stick there, all the while congratulating myself for my wise decision to stop early. Tonight will be a breeze. I'll put on dry clothes, eat a nice warm meal, and get cozy inside my fluffy down sleeping bag. I'll read my data book while listening to the rain—which is certain to return—as it taps onto my tent. I'll fall asleep with a smile on my face, then get up tomorrow and put in a long full day.

I reach the tree that I want to camp under, push off my shoulder straps and gently place the pack onto a large, low rock. I loosen the cinch at the top of the pack and stare down at my food bag. I always put my food bag on top. It's just a plastic shopping bag. By placing it on top, it's easy to get snacks out during the day, plus the food doesn't get crushed. I take a closer look and notice that the food bag is soaked. This isn't good, but no worries. It's on top and received the brunt of the rain. It didn't have the extra protection of the sturdy black trash bag. It's okay.

There's a large pocket that runs down the front of my pack, which serves as an additional buffer to the elements. I figure the rest of my gear will be dry. I pull out the dripping food bag, lay it on the rock, untie the trash bag and peer inside at the fly and tent, both of which are packed loose, not in a stuff sack. I'm surprised to see that the fly is wet. I take it out, shake the water off, and place it on the rock. I'm not sure how it got that wet but certainly the rest of my gear will be fine. I grab my tent and it, too, is soaked. No matter, a wet tent is no big deal. I can set it up and deal with it. Not a problem.

My heart rate increases as I dig deeper into the pack to the gear that does matter: pants, socks, and most importantly, my sleeping bag. A sense of horror sweeps over me as one-by-one I pull out each item and each is wet. At the very bottom of the trash bag is my sleeping bag. This is the deal breaker. My hand reaches in and touches it. My heart skips a beat. It's wet and I'm stunned. How did this happen? How can I possibly stay here tonight? What shall I do? It's getting dark. If I turn around now it will be a rigorous 10-mile hike back to the pass. I think of the forecasts blaring at me from the television this morning, shouting adamantly that the sun will not be back for a week. I feel bleak thinking about the long night that lies ahead of me. Gone is the smug feeling of making good decisions. Gone is the notion that I'm prepared for anything. It's going to be a rough night.

I pitch my tent and then blow up my air mattress, grateful that its insulation should provide some warmth. It starts to rain. I unroll my sleeping bag, happily noticing dry patches here and there, but it's at least 60% wet. I remove my wet clothes and put on the only two things that are dry: my new wool shirt and new wool socks. I slip the shirt over my head and its lovely teal color lifts my spirits. I reach for the pretty red and orange floral socks and put them on. My silk sleeping bag liner is damp, trail-worn, and in shreds but it will help. I tried to replace it in Seattle by going to, or calling, every outdoor store in the city but couldn't find a replacement. It must be a hot item in the Northwest because silk, like wool, provides warmth even when wet.

The dark night descends. I put on my headlamp and sit my chilled body on the edge of the air mattress. Clad only in shirt and socks, I cover the rest of me with me strands of silk liner and then do the only thing I can think to do next: I wrap my damp sleeping bag around me and eat an avocado.

I'm in a fix. I don't see how I can hike another 94 miles with wet gear that will only get wetter if the weatherman is right. Without the sun, nothing will dry. I'll probably be fine during the day but three more nights in a wet bag is something I'm not sure I can handle or even survive. In fact, I'm not even sure how I'm going to make it through tonight. It's getting very cold. I'll have to turn around tomorrow. I hate backtracking but there's no other way. I'll turn around, find a hotel, and dry out my gear.

I get inside my sleeping bag and try to adjust to its sogginess. After a few minutes I start shivering. This is not good. I consider hypothermia and decide to make a cup of tea. I get out of the bag, unzip the tent and boil water in the vestibule (something I don't advise, or usually do). A big cup of tea is just what is needed, that and more food. I gobble down nut bars, an apple, almond butter, salty tortilla chips, and have an oatmeal cookie with my chamomile tea. I stop shivering and get back into the bag. It feels like I've been here forever, though only an hour and a half has elapsed since my arrival. I still have ten hours to go cooped up this wet, cold tent.

Every part of me is damp but I try to get used to it. I think about the bed I slept in last night, with its fine linens and cozy comforter. The guest room at David and Katie's house in Seattle is downstairs and both nights their dog slept with me. He's a Burmese Mountain dog named Yukon, but for some reason I kept calling him Tundra. Thinking of him prompts me to sing a little tune that hasn't entered my brain in years. It goes like this: *"Who let the dogs out? Woof woof. Woof woof woof woof woof. Woof."* I sing this little ditty over and over. It's a good distraction at first, but after awhile it becomes annoying. It's too late. The song is stuck in my brain. I lie there curled up in my wet sleeping bag with this corny song stuck on auto-play. An excruciating pain shoots through my right calf. I have a Charlie horse! I reach down to soothe it but can't make the pain go away. Eventually it subsides enough so that I can gently release my calf, then the same thing happens to my other leg. I writhe in unfathomable pain. Whenever there's a slight pause from pain, the song drifts back into my mind: *"Who let the dogs out? Woof woof. Woof woof woof woof woof. Woof."* I get another Charlie horse. I have one in each leg now and am consumed in pain. The last time I had one was years ago while swimming across Walden Pond. I don't understand why I'm getting them now. It must have to do with the dampness and the cold. I force myself to drink an electrolyte solution. For the next two hours, my legs take turns cramping up while my mind relentlessly sings, *"Who Let the Dogs Out?"* I feel cursed as I fall into a light slumber. I'm not sure how long I've been asleep when something skitters across my face. What's that?

I get onto my knees, grab my headlamp, and look around.

There's a hole on the side of my tent the size of a golf ball. As I'm pondering this, a mouse jumps out from underneath my mat and I let out a blood-curdling scream. Honestly, this is no ordinary scream. It has guttural depth and infinite reach and scares even me. I'm certain that it's penetrating back through the ages, curling the toes of all my dead ancestors. The mouse doesn't like it much either. In fact, it looks like I may have given it a heart attack. The little monster was climbing his way up the mesh door of my tent, just inches from my nose, when I let loose with the scream. Now he's hanging there paralyzed with his long white tail dangling in front of me. There's only one thing to do. I grab his stringy tail, unzip the tent door, and throw him out. If you're a tough guy who does this stuff all the time or if you've walked the Appalachian Trail and are used to mice, then this scene is no big deal. To me, it's a unique new horror. Given the circumstances of the evening, I'm not pleased. How much more of this can I take? For the first time in over 2,400 miles, I've had enough. I want to quit the trail. Curiosity? I don't think so. Desire? Not right now.

But I do have to pee. The chamomile tea I had earlier is exploding in my bladder. It's raining hard and I don't want to go out, so I do something that I do every now and then. It's a dirty little secret. I grab my titanium coffee cup, place it strategically under me and do my business. I do this while poised over my sleeping bag which is a strategic error because when I move, the whole thing spills onto the inside of my bag. I can't believe it! The night cannot possibly get worse. Not only is my bag wet, it reeks of urine and is sticky. Verdict is in. I'm done. I'm quitting the trail. I can't do this anymore. I've had enough. At first light, I'll pack up and head down to the pass and be done with it! Who needs this? *Who does this anyway? And why?* Yes, it has been an astonishing journey. Yes, I've met amazing people, seen incredible things and pushed myself beyond my limits. I've been outdoors 24/7—exactly what I've always wanted to do—exactly what I've always needed to do, but it's over. Who cares if I walk 2,650 miles or 2,450 miles? Who needs Canada? I have stories galore—each day is a story; each moment is a story. Canada was only a goal, never the point. I've had enough. Tomorrow I'll pack up and go home. Good riddance. I'm tired. Enough already.

I hunker down in my bag with my nose poking out so that I can breathe and fall back to sleep. Who let the dogs out? Woof.

September 21

I wake to a strange glow inside my tent. It confuses me until I realize that this strange yellow light is the sun. I push my soggy, lumpy, urine-stained bag off my body and leap outside. There she is: the morning star. The sun goddess has made an appearance and her luminous touch has reached me. Instantly my firm decision to leave the trail disintegrates. How can things change so fast? The tortuous night is over with only a few harsh reminders: holes in my tent, wet gear, and physical exhaustion. I pack up. Maybe the weather pattern is shifting? It's worth taking a chance.

I get back on the trail and walk with my sleeping bag draped around my shoulders, hoping it will dry. The sun dodges in and out of thick grey clouds. A dozen miles later, I enter the Glacier Peak Wilderness Area, and am in awe. This is some of the most spectacular landscape my heart has ever felt. Snow-covered peaks, wide sweeping valleys, steep ravines, and boisterous creeks envelop me. At noon the sun arrives in full force, burning away every trace of bad weather, replacing it with warmth and a deep blue sky. I climb onto a huge boulder, empty my pack and turn my sleeping bag inside out, letting the sun sanitize it. I stay here for well over an hour lunching on orange slices, chocolate, and cheese. When even my thick wool socks are dry, I move on.

I walk to the top of a long gentle slope and see a bear in the distance eating berries. If I keep going, I'll have to pass him. He doesn't see or sense me. I'm downwind and he's too engrossed with his berries. I take a good look around. This could be Switzerland. I'm high above tree line with crazy-beautiful, snow-covered mountains nearby. Why go anywhere? Why not stay here forever? I've taken several breaks already today and need to clock some miles. To alert the bear of my presence, I start singing as loud as I can (if you must know, "Blue Skies" not, "Who Let the Dogs Out?"). He doesn't flinch. But I keep at it until the plump 'ole bruin finally notices me and scurries away. I hike nonstop for the rest of the day. The sun sets and the full moon rises, lingering above a shadowy horizon before sliding into a tangle of pinkish-purple clouds. A lavender hue is cast onto the earth, onto shrubs, and onto me. The clouds separate and the moon appears, bright and alone. This is the fifth and final full moon of my walk. I bow to my graceful, lunar companion. I bow to this arduous journey. I bow to the pulsating earth at my feet. I bow to life.

The light shifts from dusk to dark as I create my home for the night, sheltered on one side by a few dwarf trees, and on the other by a steep drop off. It's a spectacular mountain home. I can practically kiss the sky. My world today was wild and raw. The sun was warm. The terrain big, wide, and varied. I saw a bear. We both ate berries. I dried all my gear.

I cook a warm pot of couscous, adding extra garlic and oil, and then sit inside my tent with the fly peeled back, sipping tea, and watching the night. Last night feels surreal. How can such a night

Glacier Peak Wilderness Area

Home for the night.

give way to such a day? If I'd left the trail, I would have missed all this. And what about tomorrow? What exotic things lie ahead for me to discover? This morning, a few rays of early morning light changed everything. If it weren't for that, I'd be on my way back to Boston. I want to remember that hell and heaven can be separated by something as simple as a thin ray of light. I want to remember that the difficult and the sublime can sit side-by-side. I wonder if I will?

September 22

I sleep long, deeply, and peacefully. My water bottles freeze during the night, although I remain warm and dry. The morning sun streams into my tent and onto me. All is right with the world.

I walk above tree line for a few hours then dip into a series of lush, green meadows that gradually lead to a dark, moist forest floor. I walk for miles in a low, dim forest flooded with thousands of mushrooms. They grow with wild abandon—huge feathery mushrooms clinging to tree trunks; tiny bright orange ones that look like tacks pushed into the earth; red-spotted mushrooms imbedded in rock. They grow on everything, in every form, and I can't stop photographing them. I climb out of the dark, damp mushroom universe into a golden field glossed with soft, late afternoon light.

I meet a woman from Nebraska hiking south. She's hoping to make it through the Sierras before it snows. Time is not on her side. Shortly after saying good-bye, she runs back up the trail with my fleece ear band. I'm grateful she took the time to do this because I would have sorely missed it. The nights have turned significantly colder. I wear it when I sleep. I continue to climb, then traverse the side of a long ridge. There are wide fields on both sides of the trail with possible good campsites, but I keep going until dark. I find a site that I like on the other side of Fire Creek. It's beside the woods and not visible from the trail. I set up fast, as it's already very cold.

Yesterday I hiked 20 miles and today 25. I'm ready for sleep. I listen as a critter moves around outside my tent. It doesn't sound small like a mouse. It's bigger—perhaps a deer? I also hear rushing water from the creek. I roll onto my right side because I don't hear well out of my left ear and it's time to stop listening to the night. I put the critter and the creek out of my mind and fall off to sleep.

It's an extremely cold night. I wake many times to pull my bag tightly around my body in order to eliminate cold air pockets; and to cinch the top of the bag, smaller and smaller, until there's an opening only the size of a quarter.

September 23

I wake up and peer outside. It's snowing! My water bottle has ice in it but it's not completely frozen. I'm warm and cozy and don't want to move. When I was in Seattle I whittled down my clothing and gear to a bare minimum to make my pack super-light. Because of this, in order to be warm I either need to be moving or need to be in my sleeping bag. This makes getting up in the morning tricky.

I brew coffee and hustle to get the tent down. I sip the coffee as I hike, watching as snow accumulates. After fifteen minutes my feet are painfully cold. I don't want to stop but I have to take care of this problem. I unlace my left shoe, pull out my foot, wrap it in a piece of shredded silk liner, and shove it back into the shoe. I do the same with my right foot. When both feet are warm, I enjoy walking in the snow, which turns to rain a few miles later.

I pass beautiful Mica Lake nestled in among rocks. I'll be done with the trail soon and have been thinking about life off-trail. As

I pass Mica Lake, I promise myself that I'll get a kitten when I get home (I've never had one) and name him after this lake.

Mica Lake

I take a sharp turn and nearly bump into a huge bear! He's eating berries. He stops to look up at me. He's bigger than the bear I saw yesterday. I freeze. It doesn't occur to me to sing to this bear. What occurs to me is to leave. I turn slowly to my right and slip down the embankment to the creek below. I slosh through the creek and up to the trail. The bear doesn't budge. He watches me until I'm almost out of sight, then turns to eat more berries.

My next and final stop before Canada is Stehekin. I know nothing about Stehekin except that it has a post office with a package waiting for me. I'm guessing it will be like my three previous stops—Walker Pass, Snoqualamie Pass, and Steven's Pass—each of them not much more than a rest area on the side of a busy road.

I have tortilla chips and dehydrated beans for dinner, then put on my headlamp and walk. I ration four butterscotch drops over the course of the next two hours, allowing myself one every 30 minutes.

The terrain is steep and choked with vegetation. There are no decent places to camp. I hike on and on. I'm happy to be clocking extra miles, yet eager to find a place to crash. The moon is hidden behind thick clouds, which makes for a black night. I hike up, down, and around dark ravines, hearing only the sound of light rain on leaves. It feels mysterious inside this foggy wilderness, alone with occasional bright eyes glowing at me from the woods.

I arrive at an established campsite near Miner's Creek. Three mice greet me by jumping around at my feet. Oh my, this again? The mice are very bold. They want food and I want sleep. I hang my pack with the food bag in it, on a tree. As I prepare to sleep, I hear mice outside my tent but am too tired to care.

September 24

Granite peaks escort me down an enchanting valley, and beyond to a place called High Bridge. The bridge crosses a wide, vivacious river. There's a picnic table with four people seated on it. They're waiting for the bus. I sit with them until the apple-red bus arrives. It takes us ten miles west, to Stehekin, where there's a lodge (very unassuming), a tiny p.o. (overflowing with character), an extremely tiny store (expensive and not stocked for hikers), and a small campground (maybe a dozen sites). Though what's most striking about Stehekin, is Lake Chelan. It's 50.5 miles long, 1.5 miles wide, 1500 feet deep, and utterly captivating. I'm smitten. It's love at first sight.

Stehekin is not just a rest area on the side of a road. It's located in North Cascades National Park and is truly a sight to behold. I have dinner at the lodge with eight other PCTers then camp a stone's throw away from the lake, and watch moonlight dance on the placid water. I'm not planning to take a zero day tomorrow, but am wooed and charmed by the moon-splashed night and decide to stay an extra day. It's simply too splendid to leave.

September 25

I receive my food package and am less than thrilled. I pick through the assortment of peanut butter, trail bars, ramen, raisins, and tea. I'm tired of this food. None of it appeals to me. Luckily, I also received a package from a friend in Maine. She sent homemade Welsh Cakes, which are dense biscuits the size of English muffins, jammed with currents. I buy a stick of butter to smear on them later.

I think about my trail friend Fat Chance. She got as far as Stehekin last year and was stopped by snow. I consider yesterday morning's snowstorm and wonder if snow will also stop me.

I head over to an all-you-can-eat buffet at a lovely rustic resort to stock up on calories. I walk up the long driveway and relax on the lawn, organizing my gear one last time before dinner. The buffet is outstanding. I eat with the knowledge that I don't like the food in my pack and consume way too much. When I'm done gorging, I don't feel so good.

My plan is to walk back to the trail after dinner but I can barely move and my stomach hurts. Maybe if I start walking, I'll feel better. After a mile, I still feel awful. I find a field near the dirt road we bumped over yesterday in the red bus. From my window seat I saw bears splashing in the river across the road from where I'm now camped. They weren't grizzlies so I advise myself to relax.

September 26
Oddly, I wake up with an enormous appetite. I have Earl Gray tea and Welsh Cakes slathered with butter for breakfast. Oh, what a delight! It's the perfect hiking food.

I get back on the trail and navigate around fresh plops of berry-filled bear scat. Some of the plops are on the trail, some beside the trail. They're everywhere. I expect to run into a bear, but instead meet a young married couple and their infant. They met while thru-hiking a few years ago and were stopped by snow. They plan to finish the trail when their baby is older.

It's Monday and I'm 78 miles from the finish. If snow doesn't get me, I should be done by Wednesday. My goal for today is to hike to Rainy Pass. I walk most of the day in a light mist and at twilight arrive at the rainless pass. I cross the road to the trailhead parking lot (a common sight at trail / road intersections). The trail leads up to Cutthroat Pass. Who names these places? I look around for a spot to camp. There are five cars in the lot. I walk by a brand new Jeep. The windows are smashed and the car has been vandalized.

I cross back over the road to a desolate campground. The dark empty sites spook me. I feel perfectly comfortable camping alone in the wild but not comfortable camping alone in quasi-civilization, near a vandalized car. I pitch my tent under an information kiosk, which isn't great either. But I feel less spooked here and the kiosk will help keep my tent dry should it rain. Once I'm settled-in for the night, I hear a strange ear-piercing screech from the dark forest.

What could that be? A bird? A distressed animal? I listen to its shrill whine all night.

Welsh Cakes

4C Flour, 1C Sugar, 1 Tsp Salt, 1 Tsp Nutmeg, 2 Sticks Butter, 2 Eggs, ⅔C Milk, 1 Tbs Vanilla, 1C Currents and if you dare, 2 cloves chopped garlic

Mix dry ingredients. Melt butter and add remaining ingredients to dry mix. Separate into four sections. Roll out, ¼" thick, cut out with a cup. Put in an un-greased skillet and cook for 5 – 8 minutes.

September 27

There are two kinds of passes: high mountain roads (like Rainy Pass), and high mountain trail passes (like Cutthroat Pass). From here to Canada there's only one more road pass, but many more trail passes. At Cutthroat Pass, twisted, rust-colored ridges extend as far as the eye can see and clouds cling to high peaks. I have breakfast while drinking in the view, then spend the entire day walking up and down long grades. I ford icy-cold creeks, and inhale the scent of damp musty earth.

By late afternoon, the rain is back and a fierce wind kicks in. I climb toward a high ridge via dozens of long switchbacks. The wind is incredibly strong. My umbrella gets blown inside out. It takes enormous energy to push through the wind. The data book describes this ridge as "viewful" but right now it's socked in with fog. I walk to the north end of the ridge. There's a steep drop to my left and a gentle slope to my right. The wind is relentless. I batten down the tent with football-sized rocks. I skip dinner and spend the night listening to my tent getting pushed around by the tempest.

September 28, 29

I wake to the sound of profound silence and step outside. The sky is clear. A hawk soars in the ravine below, while mountains spill endlessly before me. The guidebook is right. It's viewful. I walk downhill, amid meadows and streams. At Hart's Pass (the last road pass) there's a large white tent with a note taped to it stating that thru-hikers can use it. I bet it looks like a sweet haven at the end of a long, rainy, windy day. It would've looked good to me last night!

There are two surveyors at the remote narrow road and they offer to take a picture for me. The moment I return to the trail the cold rain and bone-chilling wind return as well. After a few hours, I see a yurt—oh, how excellent it will be to dry off and have lunch there. I make my way over to it but it's locked. There's no way to get in. I need to stop someplace out of the rain to eat and drink something warm. I squat beside a fir tree and lean over my stove. Cold rain drips inside my collar and down my back. I eat fast, feel better, and hike without stopping for the rest of the afternoon.

After walking 20 miles, I calculate that it's only another 17 miles to the border! For the first time in 124 days of walking, I finally, really, truly, believe that I'm going to finish. I honestly didn't believe it until now. When I met people and they said, "You're almost there, you're almost done! Congratulations!" My knee-jerk response was always, "Not there yet. Anything can happen between here and the finish." But now I'm so close I can smell it, and the scent makes me hungry. A surge of energy swells through my body, and my mind starts to reel. I'm stopped in a low, musky basin having coffee. I want to finish. It's five o'clock and I've hiked 20 miles. If I hike two miles an hour for the next seven hours I can add 14 miles to the day and be three miles from the border when I wake up tomorrow. There are rugged mountain passes ahead, plus the dark night will slow me. I rationalize that hiking into the wee hours on my last full day on the trail will be a sweet way to end my journey. I'm going for it! For an extra push, I suck down another cup of java and am happily enthusiastic about my plan to hike until 2:00 a.m.!

I leave the basin and climb for an hour until breaking out onto a high plateau, sparsely dotted with scrub pines and low bushes. A steep, exposed rocky ridge lies beyond the plateau. The trail is carved into its side. After that, there'll be a steep descent and then a climb up to Woody Pass. I stumble on a rock and when I lift my gaze from the ground, I see a man up ahead. Who could this be? He has long brown hair and a messy beard. He moves slowly until he sees me, then he hunches down and runs. As he scampers across the plateau I instinctively wave. He ignores me and ducks into the bushes. Strange. I was happy to see him because I thought he must be another thru-hiker. I haven't seen another backpacker since Stehekin. I wonder who he is? I have a sense of who's ahead of me on the trail and a sense of who may be a day or two behind. I don't understand where this guy fits into the equation.

Who is he? Why is he hiding? I walk until I'm just a few yards from where he fled into the brush. I walk off-trail instead of passing directly beside the area where he is hiding. It's all very strange. I begin to traverse the side of the ridge, glancing down every now and then looking for him. It's disconcerting knowing that I'm in his line of sight and that he's probably tracking my every step. For the first time since the Mexican border, I feel uncomfortable on the trail due to the presence of another human being. I can think of nothing else.

The border isn't far away and it's unmanned. It's simply a thin path uniting the U.S. to Canada. There are no border patrols, no inspections, no passports required, and no steel wall. If someone wanted to sneak into this country it would be a good place to do it, and late at night would be a good time to try. Maybe the guy hiding in the bushes has friends coming to meet him tonight? My plan to hike until 2:00 a.m. on a desolate path in the middle of nowhere, no longer sounds like a good idea.

I hustle across the exposed ridge as fast as I can, and when I'm out of view I re-think the situation. Is my imagination getting carried away? Is the thought of coming face-to-face with an unsavory character an irrational fear or a possible reality? Either way, the plan doesn't feel right anymore.

After sunset, I walk for two hours in dark fog, then camp on a rocky ridge far from the path and far from any possible encounters. I have noodles with capers, olive oil, and raisins for my last meal on the trail. The night air is extremely cold. The fog dissipates, as do my fears. I keep my tent door open, watching the night sky one last time. After months of living in the wild, this curious journey will soon be over. I'm thin and tired and always hungry but I feel strong. I've found ways to adjust to the natural world, and to cold, rainy Washington. Its weather is a small price to pay for the gift of immersing myself in this wondrous state.

A part of me is ready to finish tomorrow. That part of me is ready for undisturbed sleep in a comfortable bed, ready to nourish my body with unlimited supplies of fresh fruits and vegetables, ready to have a more extensive wardrobe, and more than ready to be with loved ones. Another part of me wants to walk to the Arctic Circle.

I nod off to sleep. My last night morphs into a clear morning with an electric-blue sky. I take my time packing, estimating that I'm nine or ten miles from the border.

I walk fast, eager to knock off the final miles. I hear footsteps from behind and turn to see a short, stocky guy named Stucco running toward me. We met once near Tahoe. When he catches up, we walk and gab all the way to the border. We reach the monument that signifies the end of the trail. Stucco flips it open and pulls out the logbook. As I sign my name, my eyes well up with emotion. Stucco notices and implores, "*Please don't cry! Because if you do, I will too, and I don't want to cry!*" I comply by putting away my tears and taking out my camera instead. We toast with some sort of disgusting alcoholic mixture that he generously offers to share. The long walk is over. It's 10:15 in the morning, September 29th, 2010. Stucco doesn't have a passport. He turns around to walk to the nearest road, 40 miles south. I continue north for another eight miles under the bluest of blue skies, to Manning Park, where I spend a sleepless night in a warm, comfortable bed.

September 30

I'm standing in line at the border, waiting to get back into the United States. Unlike the remote border I crossed yesterday, this one has officials. The air is thick with tension, as it always seems to be when going through customs. Suddenly it occurs to me— oh no!—they're going to ask me what the purpose of my visit to Canada was. I feel the tears that I didn't get to have yesterday morning return. And again, I push them away.

The burly officer in his late-thirties shouts "*Next!*" as he waves me over toward him. When I hand him my passport he asks, "What was the purpose of your visit to Canada?" Honestly, I try hard—so very hard—but I can't help but tremble. My eyes water up as I hear myself say, "I walked here. I walked to Canada. I walked to Canada from Mexico on the Pacific Crest Trail." He asks a lot of questions about the trail. How long did it take? What was the most beautiful part? Was it hard? Are you glad you did it? When he's done with his questions I get back onto the bus.

PCT Monument

October 3

I've been in Seattle three days. It feels strange to be back in this world, knowing that my long walk is over and that I won't be returning to the wilderness. I've been sleeping in a warm bed, eating an abundance of fresh food, taking baths, and talking at length with friends. Everything looks and feels like I'm experiencing it for the very first time. I wasn't gone that long. Why does it feel this way? The phrase "*everything and nothing has changed*" keeps coursing through my brain.

Remember the great blue heron I saw months ago in the desert? It was an unusual habitat for that bird. I saw it shortly after my mom's death and it reminded me of her. I never saw another heron until just moments before reaching Manning Park. I was in the woods. Out of the corner of my eye I saw something move. I turned to see a great blue heron standing in a small pool of water. She noticed me. Our eyes met. Then she lifted her body out of the water and into the clear Canadian sky.

Heron Rises from the Dark, Summer Pond
By Mary Oliver, WHAT DO WE KNOW

So heavy
is the long-necked, long-bodied heron,
always it is a surprise
when her smoke-colored wings

open
and she turns
from the thick water,
from the black sticks

of the summer pond,
and slowly

About the Author

ANNE ELIZABETH O'REGAN lives in New England with her partner Bruce, and their cat Mica. She is currently working on her next book entitled, *The Bear That Followed Me Home*. To order more books, or to contact Anne, please email her at: aeoregan8@gmail.com

Washington

rises into the air
and is gone.

Then, not for the first or the last time,
I take the deep breath
of happiness, and I think
how unlikely it is

that death is a hole in the ground,
how improbable
that ascension is not possible,
though everything seems so inert, so nailed

back into itself—
the muskrat and his lumpy lodge,
the turtle,
the fallen gate.

And especially it is wonderful
that the summers are long
and the ponds so dark and so many,
and therefore it isn't a miracle

but the common thing,
this decision,
this trailing of the long legs in the water
this opening up of the heavy body

into a new life: see how the sudden
gray-blue sheets of her wings
strive toward the wind; see how the cla
takes her in.